Waste: Discussing Health Insurance As a Social Security of the Waste Pickers

-Daniyal Jadhav

ACKNOWLEDMENT

At the very outset I would like to my Parents, my sister Dr Kannamal Jadhav, my aunt Dr. Shamal Jadhav and my Uncles; Mr. Rajaram Jadhav and; Mr. Subhash Sasane, for the blessings and support they have given me throughout this journey.

I also express my wholehearted gratitude to Dr. Shashikala Gurpur, Director; Symbiosis Law School, Pune; Dean, Faculty of Symbiosis International University and Mrs. Lasya Vyakranam, Assistant Professor Symbiosis Law School, Pune for always being a source of my strength and extending a helping hand to me.

Lastly, I would be failing in my duty if I didn't extend this endeavour to my friends Shruti, Dagle, Neeraj, Omkar, Atul, Manoj, Saish, Divyansha, Shashank, Prasanna and Kedar who have been my constant source of unwavering support and without whose cooperation, this would not have been possible.

DANIYAL CHANDRAWADAN JADHAV

CHAPTER 1

HEALTH INSURANCE AS SOCIAL SECURITY OF UNORGANISED SECTOR IN MAHARASHTRA: THE CASE STUDY OF THE RAGPICKERS

INTRODUCTION

Indian economy is primarily divided into 3 sectors namely: Primary, Secondary, and Tertiary. In terms of the operation, it is divided into the organised sector and the unorganised sector; whereas in terms of ownership it is divided into the public sector and private sector.[1] The Indian economy is characterised as a developing market economy. The organised sector consists of the formal labour class, also called the licensed organisations. These are those workers who are registered and pay taxes to the government; which includes people working in public traded companies, corporation, factories, shopping malls, hotels, and large business.[2] The unorganised sector consists of the informal labour class which is also called unlicensed organisations or self-employed. This includes handicrafts and handloom workers or rural traders or other labours that are described by ILO under the unorganised sector.[3]

---

[1] Gender Dimensions of the Informal Sector and Informal Employment in India Page no. 2-3 (July.18,2020, 11:20 PM), GLOBAL FORUM ON GENDER STATISTICS ESA/STAT/AC.168/41 26-28 January 2009
https://unstats.un.org/unsd/gender/Ghana_Jan2009/Doc41.pdf

[2] Ibid, Page no. 2

[3] The ILO and the Informal Sector an institutional history, Page no. 9

The term *informal sector* was first used by International Labour Organisation i.e. ILO, which defined "informality as a way of doing things characterised by (a) easy of entry; (b) reliance of indigenous resources: (c) family ownership; (d) small scale operations; (e) labour-intensive and adaptive technology; (e) skills acquired outside of the formal sector; (g) unregulated and competitive markets."[4] According to NCEUS unorganised sector is defined as "The unorganised sector consists of all unincorporated private enterprises owned by individuals or households engaged in the sale and production of goods and services operated on a proprietary or partnership basis and with less than ten total workers."[5]

70% of the Indian population lives in rural areas and their primary source of livelihood is agriculture which nearly contributes 50% of India GDP.[6][7] Indian economy consists of approximately 10% of the organised sector,[8] while the unorganised sector or informal sector constitutes a pivotal part of the Indian economy i.e. more than 90% of people are working in the unorganised sector of the country.[9][10] The main reason for this

---

[4] Paul E. Bangasser, The ILO and the informal sector: an institutional history, ISBN-92-2-112243-3

[5] Reports on Financing of Enterprises in the Unorganised Sector & Creation of a National Fund for the unorganised sector (NAFUS), National Commission for Enterprises in the Unorganised Sector, Page no. 3

[6] Fact book CIA 2018-2014

[7] Supra Note 5, page no 91

[8] India Brand Equity Foundation, Economic Survey 2018-2019, (Jan.18,2020 12:20 PM).https://www.ibef.org/economy/economic-survey-2018-19.

disproportionality is the lack of skill or education among the workers of the unorganised sector. In order to work in the organised sector, one needs to have the desired skills and basic education which is lacking among the people of this sector. Due to the unavailability of work, these people migrate to the urban areas for employment which results in the addition of unorganised workers. Thus, the unorganised sector is the major sector contributing to the gross domestic product of the country; and can easily be seen in both rural and urban areas.

A majority of workers in this sector neither receive many facilities or benefits by the government nor do they have any fixed employee-employer relationship. Most of the people in this working-class do not have any association or unions which can represent them or fight for their rights. The workers in this sector can be seen doing the risky and unhygienic job which leads to infections, contaminations and bad health conditions. Owing to these conditions, they end up spending their daily wages in hospitals which generally brings them poverty and economic vulnerability.[11] They do not get the benefit of governmental welfare schemes like pension, maternity benefits or other old-age benefits.[12] These are the reasons why these workers are usually

---

[9] Ibid

[10] Supra Note 5, page no 91

[11] The Challenge of Employment in India An Informal Economy Perspective Volume I - Main Report
NATIONAL COMMISSION FOR ENTERPRISES IN THE UNORGANISED SECTOR , Page No. 3

found selling their assets or often found borrowing money from moneylenders with high interests at the time of paying hospital bills.

However, to overcome this problem Central government and Maharashtra state government have taken various initiatives; one of them is by introducing health insurance schemes for the people working in the unorganised sector. There are various health insurance schemes which are currently active like MJPJAY, PMJAY, Trust hospitals, etc which are run by the government in Maharashtra. Though these schemes are active, the poor people are unable to obtain the benefit from them, or unwilling to have health insurance because of its cost, lack of perceived benefits or lack of awareness.

Rag pickers are the class of the workers in the unorganised sector, who play an important part in the Indian economy. The term *ragpicker* currently refers to people who collect rags or recyclable materials that can be sold for money. 'Rag-picking entails the sorting, collecting, and selling of these various waste materials that can be found at dumpsites, riverbanks, street corners, or in residential areas, and consist primarily of plastics, bottles, cardboard, tin, aluminium, iron, brass, and copper.' The products of plastic, tin and aluminium are heavily sought while papers stand low on the list. This is done because the ragpickers get paid

---

[12]Ibid , Page No 4

according to the quality of the materials they sell to junkyards and garbage collection centres.[13]

Rag pickers often work alone, seeking the financial value of the recyclable elements to sell or use. They are usually unequipped to disassemble the products they find on the dumpsites. The garbage thrown on the dumpsites causes pollution and poisons their bodies. Ragpickers require environmental shields and tools for appropriately disassembling the products and should be trained to only focus on products they can effectively disassemble properly with these tools.[14] These people contribute a major part in the Indian economy as they collect scrap, waste and recyclable material that contribute to the welfare environment and the economy of the country. It was also declared by the Indian government that there will be a prize for the best ragpicker in India.

"As a response to poverty and the increasing value of recyclables, the number of people involved in rag picking is growing in many cities across the globe, particularly in large metropolitan areas."[15] "The collection of recyclables is a

---

[13] International Labour Organisation International Programme on the Elimination of Child Labour (IPEC)
Investigating the Worst Forms of Child Labour No. 4 Nepal Situation of Child Ragpickers: aA Rapid Assessment, Page no. 8

[14] Ibid Page no. 9

[15] International Labour Organisation International Programme on the Elimination of Child Labour (IPEC)
Investigating the Worst Forms of Child Labour No. 4 Nepal Situation of Child

widespread activity among urban poor, particularly in countries with large socio-economic disparities. The health of Ragpickers is at risk because of unsafe working conditions, socio-economic exclusion, and stigmatisation."[16] To protect this class of the society, the government has taken a lot of initiatives and has offered them a helping hand in monetary terms by providing them with various insurance schemes.

Insurance is risk management under which an insurer on premium undertakes to eliminate or reduce risk of life or property.[17] The insurance can be described as a device which is used to reduce or eliminate the risk of loss to life and property and provides financial support, safety and security against a particular event.[18]

Insurances are also provided by the government free of cost or sometimes at a nominal charge. "Insurance generates a significant impact on the economy by mobilising domestic savings. Insurance turns accumulated capital into productive investments.[19] Insurance enables to mitigate loss, provides financial stability, and promotes trade and commerce activities which results in economic growth and development."[20] Thus, insurance has become an

---

Ragpickers: A Rapid Assessment, Page no. 8
[16] Ibid, Page no. 9
[17] General principles of law of insurance Page no. 9; R.N.Chaudhary
[18] Ibid Page no. 7
[19] R-money, Importance of Insurance-You must Know (July.18,2020, 11:20 PM), https://rmoneyinsurance.com/blogs/life-insurance/importance-insurance-must-know.
[20] Government Insurance versus Market Insurance Author(s): George L. Priest Source: The Geneva Papers on Risk and Insurance. Issues and Practice, Vol. 28,

important source of capital formation. The government is also benefited by providing insurance to the general public.

Providing insurances will benefit the Rag pickers in a very efficient way, as most of the ragpickers hail from economically backward sections and are not educated or aware. It is common for them to ignore the small-time health problems like fever, cold, body pain, etc which can lead to prolonged diseases.[21] Therefore, providing social security to ragpickers and spreading awareness of such services should be the major concern of the government.

---

[21] International Labour Organisation International Programme on the Elimination of Child Labour (IPEC) Investigating the Worst Forms of Child Labour No. 4 Nepal Situation of Child Ragpickers: A Rapid Assessment , Page no. 11-12

CHAPTER 2

IMPORTANCE OF THE RAGPICKERS IN INDIAN ECONOMY AND THE NEED OF SOCIAL SECURITY.

INTRODUCTION

Waste production and consumption are one of the nature's basic laws. The biological wastes are the basic part of the planet earth, but the man made waste materials like plastic, industrial waste and now e-waste is changing the structure of the natural eco-system and it's functioning. With the advent of the industrial revolution and the rapid advancements in the automobile industry, waste consumption per capita began increasing in an accelerated manner.[22] 'In the Indian scenario, the so-called waste pickers, who come from highly vulnerable social backgrounds, play a unique role in collecting those wastes.' Waste pickers or rag-pickers; bring out their living by collecting and selling recyclable materials out of municipal solid wastes in the urban counterpart of the human settlements. In this process, they make a significant contribution to the environmental management in different metropolis over and above rendering a service to the local economy. This chapter

---

[22]Ar. Jepranshu Aganivanshi, The Rag Pickers and the Urban Economy – A Case Study of Seemapuri region, Delhi, International Journal of Research in Social Sciences, ISSN: 2249-2496

mainly deals with the Ragpickers in India and their need for health insurance. It includes their problems, health hazards and risks in their work and at the end concludes with how they play an important role in the Indian Economy.

2.1 HISTORY OF RAG-PICKING

Colombian history says that the recycling activity started around the 1930's due to internal politics and socio-economical problems. The war in Colombia forced displacement from rural to urban areas. When these people arrived in the cities with their children and animals in search of food and shelter, they landed up in the dumpsites. It has also been found out that recyclers in the big cities were former peasants and therefore the life in the city breaks their whole economic rationality. These people used to get food from the dump yards and they traded by the barter system. At the same time, the new kinds of wastes which were produced started being a problem and the only solution was to gather it and to make it disappear by throwing it into the rivers. The growing number of dumpsites created an opportunity for this displaced population. They started to search and collect wastes which could recover them some food. The increasing demand from the medical companies and pharmaceutical companies initiated the recycling activities. The need for small glass bottles for different purposes, created an opportunity for the waste pickers.[23]

2.2 RAGPICKERS IN INDIA

Rag pickers are one of the organised – unorganised labour classes of the country, who play an important role in the economy of India. Rag-picking occupation mainly deals with the collection of rags or recyclable material which has an exchange value.

The SWM Rules define a 'waste picker' under Rule 3(1)(58): 'as a person or groups of persons informally engaged in collection and recovery of reusable and recyclable solid waste from the source of waste generation the streets, bins, material recovery facilities, processing and waste disposal facilities for sale to recyclers directly or through intermediaries to earn their livelihood.' "Rag pickers are broadly divided into three categories:

- *Itinerant rag pickers*, who mainly pick up recyclables from streets, dump sites and businesses but not residences;
- *Fixed Rag pickers*, who have been formally integrated into the door to door waste collection programmes run by municipalities; and,
- *Itinerant Buyers*, who purchase recyclables from the waste pickers and then resell them up the chain for an added value,"[24]

---

[23] Deutsche Gesellschaft für, Internationale Zusammenarbeit (GIZ) GmbH Postfach 518065726 , Eschborn/Germany,Recovering resources, creating opportunities Integrating the informal sector into solid waste management ;By Silvio Ruiz, Coordinator of the Recyclers 'Asociación ARB (Asociación de Recicladores de Bogotá)

[24] Akhileshwar reddy, Alok Prasanna Kumar, Waste pickers welfare law in Karnataka, vidhilegalpolicy.in

Rag picking occupation is mainly adopted by the population which is dislocated or migrated from rural to urban areas in search of shelter and livelihood.[25] As per the *All India Kabadi Mazdoor Mahasangh*, there are 40 lakhs ragpickers in India out of which five lakhs are in Delhi alone.[26] This profession is mainly adopted by the females and according to the reports, there are 73% women working in the waste picking sector.[27] Rag-picking is also dominated by the children ageing 5-17 years who do not have other skills and thus by adopting this profession contributes to their family.[28] About 90% of the ragpickers are found illiterate and their children are mostly engaged in the same occupation.[29] Children engaged in rag picking are victims of discrimination in schools and are often ill-treated by teachers and privileged children because of the social stigma attached to their work and their dirty clothes. Even the children enrolled in schools continue to work as rag pickers and are often absent or come late

---

[25] G. Siva Praveena Ch. Durga Prasad Prof. P.V.V. Prasada Rao, The Plight of Rag-pickers at Dump yard Socio - Economic Profile a Case Study of Visakhapatnam, ISSN: 2454-5988, Cointreau, Sandra. 2006. "Occupational and Environmental Health Issues of Solid Waste Management: Special Emphasis on Middle and Lower-Income Countries." Urban Papers 2, World Bank, Washington, DC. Dhuy, Eloise. 2008.

[26] Shreyasee Raj, Oct 30, 2019,(May.04,2020, 01:20 AM), https://www.indiatimes.com/news/india/ragpickers-are-our-unsung-heroes-in-keeping-india-clean-high-time-govt-starts-caring-for-them-378820.htm.

[27] Ujwala Samarth for KKPKP, The Occupational Health of Waste Pickers in Pune: KKPKP and SWaCH Members Push for Health Rights

[28] Bhaskar Majumder, & G. Rajvanshi, migrating to rag picking: unfolding some facts about child rag picking in Allahabad, Uttar Pradesh.

[29] Supra Note 27, Ujwala Samarth

to the school. Their concentration in studies is reduced due to their working conditions.[30]

Ragpickers are the poor class of the society and their earning depends upon the rag or the material they collect. Different materials have different rates per kilograms i.e. their earning depends upon how much they collect daily or on what material they find or what type of waste they collect. According to the study conducted on various data, it is seen that ragpickers earn Rs. 175-200 per day,[31] i.e. after working for such long hours and walking miles they earn Rs. 200 per day. The Environment Minister also stated that Ragpickers of India collects nearly 22-28% of wastes in India which is processed and recycled.[32] The former Environment Minister also declared that there will be a national award i.e. prize of 1.50 lakhs for the 3 best rag pickers in India. However, there is no further confirmation for this scheme.

2.3 RAG-PICKING AND NEED of HEALTH INSURANCE

2.3. A. RAG-PICKING

---

[30] Supra Note 28, Bhaskar Majumder,& G. Rajvanshi,

[31] Rajanya Bose & Anirban Bhattacharya, Why Ragpickers, Unrecognised And Unpaid, Are Critical For Waste Management In India, May 12, 2017,(May.05,2020, 01:20 AM) indiaspend.com

[32] Ibid

The term "Rag pickers is more specifically attached to those persons who collect materials, which are usually gathered at dumpsites, riverbanks, street corners or in residential areas, and mainly consists of plastics, bottles, cardboard papers, tin, aluminium, iron, brass, copper, iron or any other material which can be recycled and exchanged by them to the junk dealer for money."[33]

The price ragpickers get for their goods varies according to the quality of the material. Different materials have different values among them. Tins, bottles, and papers are not worth much, and metal and plastic materials have a good value.[34] However, higher price materials such as copper, brass, and aluminium are hard to find, and may be assumed to be the product of theft.[35] Thus, plastics and polythene are easier and most commonly collected materials. The type of materials gathered also depends on the amount of experience of the ragpicker. Newcomers prefer to pick the materials that are easily found, such as plastics and bottles, while older ones tend to be more selective and prefer to collect

---

[33] International Labour Organization International Programme on the Elimination of Child Labour (IPEC) Investigating the Worst Forms of Child Labour No. 4 Nepal Situation of Child Ragpickers: A Rapid Assessment , Page no. 18

[34] Sarkar, Papiya"Solid Waste Management In Delhi – A Social Vulnerability Study" in Martin J. Bunch, V. Madha Suresh and T. Vasantha Kumaran, eds., Proceedings of the Third International Conference on Environment and Health, Chennai, India, 15-17 December, 2003. Chennai: Department of Geography, University of Madras and Faculty of Environmental Studies, York University. Pages 451 – 464

[35] Supra Note 31, Rajanya Bose & Anirban Bhattacharya

relatively more valuable goods such as metals and plastics over tins, bottles, or papers.[36]

2.3. B. SEASON

Rag-picking is not a seasonal occupation and the ragpickers are active in their work for all 12 months of the year. It is claimed that the market value of the rags varies due to the changing seasons, the variation of price of the recyclable materials and market value of the products. Rag picking is not a seasonal profession and they work in all seasons, but the rainy season affects their working efficiency as their working hours get reduced and most of the collectibles get soiled and devalued.[37]

A study made by Ar. *Jepranshu Aganivanshi* in Delhi, found that the ragpickers are more favoured to work after the festive seasons like Diwali and Eid as metals like bronze, brass and iron is more likely to be found after this seasons.[38] The study made by the ILO in Nepal also claimed that the ragpickers are more favoured to work in the winter season than the summer or rainy season due to the weather conditions and the market rate of the recyclable materials.[39]

---

[36] Ibid

[37] Informal Economy Monitoring Study: Waste Pickers in Pune, India ,Publication date: April 2014 ISBN number: 978-92-95095-89-2

[38] Supra Note 24, Akhileshwar Reddy, Alok Prasanna Kumar,

[39] Supra Note 31, Rajanya Bose & Anirban Bhattacharya

2.3. C. WORKING HOURS AND EARNINGS

Working for long hours is necessary for ragpickers because their earning is completely dependent on the rag they collect and the quality of the rag they pick, which depends upon the hours they work. On an average, 50% of the ragpickers work for 9-12 hours daily and 75% of them walk for more than five hours daily.[40] The majority of ragpickers do not use any vehicle for collecting rags. Ragpickers start their work early in the morning so that they don't lose their rags to their competitors. Some ragpickers work at night and mostly work in commercial areas to find good material which is disposed off after the office working hours.[41] Working hours of ragpickers vary with the change of seasons.

After long hours of working throughout the day, when the collection bag of the ragpickers is full, and they return from their work, they go to the junkyard dealer where they sell the rags. These rags have different rates for the different materials. Different cities have different rates for the materials but it does not vary much. Approximately, the material is charged from Rs. 5 per kg to Rs. 12 per kg. The rate of metals ranges between Rs.7 to Rs.12 per kg, whereas plastics, other papers and cardboard range from Rs.5

---

[40] Supra Note 27 ,Ujwala Samarth for KKPKP, Page no. 4

[41] Report on Rapid Assessment Surveyon Socio-Economic Condition of Waste Pickers in Kolkata Municipal Area, society for Direct Initiative for Social and Health Action (DISHA), (May.18,2020, 03:20 AM), www.dishaearth.org, January 2017.

to Rs.7 per kg. Thus, if a ragpicker, on average collects 40-50 kg of metal rags he earns approximately Rs. 400 per day, and if he collects paper and cardboards then he earns approximately Rs. 200 per day.[42] These are the maximum figures which a ragpicker can earn and each day is not the same for them. These figures vary daily and their earning solely depends upon what material they find and how many kilograms of waste they collect. Sometimes ragpickers do not segregate their wastes and directly sell the complete bags to the junkyard dealers. In this case, the dealer just checks the weight of the bags and pays them the money accordingly. Ragpickers that do not have the skill to segregate the material collected or do not know the cost of materials they deal with, are mostly at the monetary loss.[43]

The junkyard dealers pay the ragpickers on a daily, weekly or monthly basis.[44] The ragpickers, for whom the only source of livelihood is rag picking, want the remuneration on the same day. Most of the ragpickers depend solely on rag picking and some of them also choose to do some other work.

2.3. D . HEALTH HAZARDS

---

[42] Ibid

[43] Ibid

[44] Kuruva Syamala Devi, Arza V.V.S. Swamy, Ravuri Hema Krishna , Studies on the Solid Waste Collection by Rag Pickers at Greater Hyderabad Municipal Corporation, India

There is a reason why rag picking is considered as the worst form of labour. The risks related to health and mental conditions, as well as unexpected incidents and accidents, makes rag picking an adverse occupation. This section considers the issues related to health and hunger, the use of substances, involvement in crime, and explains the need for health insurance to the ragpickers.

Most of the ragpickers start their work at dawn and work till dusk while some of the ragpickers work from dusk to dawn. They face a lot of risks and health hazards within these hours. The major risk to the ragpickers is getting bitten by the dogs during their work hours. Ragpickers often get bitten by the dogs or pigs or other insects on the dumpsites or on the streets. 'They often get contacted with the used bandages, disposable diapers, toilet paper, sanitary napkins, disposable needles or syringes, and used condoms on the dumpsites or while collecting the rags . Besides these, the wastes from small clinics, pharmacies, labs, and even hospital wastes, may also be found mixed with residential trash, carrying micro-organisms responsible for causing more serious diseases.'[45][46]

Ragpickers often walk for a long-distance or pull heavy carts or bicycles loaded with the rags on it, which causes the musculoskeletal problems. 'The open dumpsites or dumping

---

[45] M C da Silva, A G Fassa, C E Siqueira, D Kriebel ,World at work: Brazilian ragpickers,

[46] Balu Natha Mote, Suhas Balasaheb Kadam, Shrikant Kishorrao Kalaskar, Bharat Shivajirao Thakare, Ambadas Suresh Adhav, Thirumugam Muthuvel, The Occupational and Environmental Health Hazards (Physical & Mental) Among Rag- Pickers in Mumbai Slums: A Cross-Sectional Study

grounds are the breeding grounds for the disease vectors such as flies, mosquitoes, cockroaches, rats, and other pests, which can cause diseases like typhoid, cholera, dysentery, yellow fever, encephalitis, plague, malaria, and dengue fever.'[47] Particularly during the rainy season, the water runoff and high humid conditions increase health hazards to the people working on such sites as the landfill sites are not properly maintained, and are prone to the groundwater contamination due to leachate percolation.[48] The dumping sites are not only breeding places to the insects or other pests but also to the other micro-organisms which can be seen in the soil, air or water in that area. These microorganisms are the main reasons which cause the infections.[49]

While working on these sites, ragpickers work bare feet or collects rags with bare hands and get them injured by the broken glass, sharp metals and thorns or get in contact with other microbial infectious organism which causes serious harm to them. They can cause skin diseases or some other harmful diseases which involves *Gastro Tract Infections* GITs.[50] Dumpsites can always be seen with smoke as ragpickers sometimes burns the tires or plastics to find or to collect the metal portion in them. This generates harmful

---

[47] A. Chandramohan, C. Ravichandran and V. Sivasankar. Solid waste, its health impairments and role of rag pickers in Tiruchirappalli city, Tamil Nadu, Southern India,
[48] Ibid
[49] Ibid
[50] Supra Note 44, Kuruva Syamala Devi, Arza V.V.S. Swamy, Ravuri Hema Krishna.

smokes and fumes which causes the Respiratory Tract Infections (RTIs). It is also found in the studies that the dumpsites generate some gases which are harmful when taken in through breathing. The ragpickers work in such sites.[51] Therefore, these people are always sick and are not aware of the health risk that comes with their work. They are mostly unaware about the health issues and even if they are aware in some cases, the problem of poverty does not allow them to go to the hospitals.

In a survey conducted by KKPKP in 2009-2010, the collection of data included 1,777 randomly selected women waste pickers in Pune. The study found that:

- The prevalence of specific symptoms related to asthma, namely wheezing, was high at 10 %, and a high morbidity index of TB was seen in 6.4 % of the women. This was about tuberculosis and asthma which could be related to occupational exposure.

- In the case of the gastrointestinal tract (GIT), symptoms suggestive of acid peptic disease were about 10%, and specific symptoms related to GIT were considered for morbidity index, which ranged from 10 to 15 % in both acute and chronic reporting. This also could be caused by the unhygienic conditions in which waste pickers operate.

---

[51] Ibid

- In the case of musculoskeletal problems, there were nearly 50% showing morbidity in four specific symptoms related to the overall system. Carrying heavy loads, climbing in and out of containers and garbage dumps, walking long distances, and low nutrition all contributed to the prevalence of these symptoms.
- About reproductive tract infection-related symptoms, 12 to 15 % had one symptom related to the reproductive tract. Also, overall 1/3rd of the women had at least one complaint related to menstruation.
- Among the chronic symptoms of various systems assessed, more than 70% of women had chronic musculoskeletal symptoms; 30% had symptoms related to menstruation; 25% had GIT symptoms, and 10% had RTI/STI symptoms. Interestingly, nearly 11% gave a history of chronic RTI or STI symptoms. This may be because these women are generally undernourished and more prone to infection including RTI/STI. This may possibly occur because they do not have access to bathrooms, which could affect their genital hygiene, leading to infections. The lack of access to toilets or water for washing right through the day is a major occupational health concern for the waste pickers.[52]

2.3. E. HIV AIDS AND STDs

---

[52] Supra Note 27, Ujwala Samarth

Ragpickers are also involved in sexual activities and sometimes works as the pimp, or go to the prostitutes for getting involved in sexual activities. Child ragpickers are also involved in homosexual sex and visit prostitutes.[53] Thus, ragpickers often have high chances of getting infected by STDs, HIV and AIDS disease. In the instant case, the police official asked the victim to take a bath first which led to the washing of evidence away.[54] Sometimes female ragpickers get raped and police often refuses to register the complaint.

2.3. F. HUNGER

Mostly females and children are engaged in the rag picking and a very few percentage of males are working as the ragpickers. The reason why female and children are working as ragpickers is to support the financial condition of the family or for their livelihood. Ragpickers are mostly engaged in the consumption of substances like alcohol, smoking, or tobacco.[55] Ragpickers invest their money in the consumption of these substances and spend all their earning in this which in turn makes them victims of the huger at the end of the day.[56] This type of attitude often lands this worker to borrow

---

[53] Supra Note 31, Rajanya Bose & Anirban Bhattacharya
[54] Mithilia Phadke, Times of India, Ragpickers most vulnerable to sexual assault,NGO says , Sep.2013,05:32 IST (June.01,2020, 09:23 AM) ,https://timesofindia.indiatimes.com/city/mumbai/Rag-pickers-most-vulnerable-to-sexual-assault-NGO-says/articleshow/22218955.cms
[55] Supra Note 45, M C da Silva, A G Fassa, C E Siqueira, D Kriebel.
[56] Supra Note 31, Rajanya Bose & Anirban Bhattacharya

the money from the junkyard dealer or other moneylenders which lands them in the situation of bondage labours.[57]

A study made by Bhaskar Majumdar in his paper states that most of the child ragpickers suffer from malnourishment that results in reducing the resistance capacity for various diseases. It was also found in the study that children sometimes consume those items that are non-consumable and are found in garbage which leads to stomach ache. This adversely affects the physical and mental health of the child.[58]

2.3. G. SUBSTANCE ABUSE

Ragpickers spend their hard-earned money on consumption of alcohol, tobacco, smoking, or drugs. Chewing tobacco and smoking cigarettes and weeds is very common among the ragpickers.[59] Ragpickers are also involved in the consumption of alcohol. In a study made by ILO in Nepal, it was found that children who are involved in rag-picking are also involved in gambling and drug usage. A child said in an interview that he gets injected with PETCHA (drug) before going to the work and if he does not get injected then he cannot enjoy his work. The girls get involved in sexual activities for drug abuse and sometimes work as prostitutes for getting money to buy drugs[60]. This adversely affects

---

[57] Ibid

[58] Ujwala Samarth for KKPKP, The Occupational Health of Waste Pickers in Pune: KKPKP and SWaCH Members Push for Health Rights

[59] Supra Note 45, M C da Silva, A G Fassa, C E Siqueira, D Kriebel.

the health of ragpickers. The risks faced by these workers in this sector go beyond the expectations. They also get infected with communicable diseases causing irreparable loss to their health.

2.3. H. RAGPICKERS AND THE CORONA VIRUS

The Novel virus named as Corona Virus (COVID-19) is a new health hazard in the life of the ragpickers. Rag picking community is not much educated and being unaware of the seriousness of the pandemic is still working on the field, without any protective gears.[61] Rag-picking is the occupation where they deal with the waste material in the landfills. It can be the bandages, disposed diapers, toilet paper, sanitary napkins, disposed needles or syringes, and used condoms. In addition, to these wastes from small clinics, pharmacies, and labs, and even hospital wastes, may also be found mixed with residential trash sometimes insects or the stray animals or the harmful microorganisms also add the seriousness to their work.[62][63] During the Covid 19 pandemic ragpickers are still working as the frontline health workers and are

---

[60] Supra Note 31, Rajanya Bose & Anirban Bhattacharya

[61] Aparna Agrawal, The Murky Underbelly of Sanitation During the Pandemic,06.APR,2020 (June.01,2020, 11:23 AM), https://thewire.in/rights/lockdown-delhi-ragpickers-sanitation-workers

[62] Supra Note 45, M C da Silva, A G Fassa, C E Siqueira, D Kriebel.

[63] Supra Note 46, Balu natha mote, Suhas Balashaeb kadam, Shrikant Kishorrao kalakar, Bharat Shivajirao Thakare, Ambadas Suresh Adhav, Thirumugam Muthuthuvel,

dealing with the used masks, PPE kits, used protective gears or empty sanitizer bottles, which are used by general public or small hospitals.[64] While dealing with such harmful viruses and while working on the landfills ragpickers don't have any protective gears or masks or sanitizers to protect them from this harmful virus.

'WHO experts Mike Ryan declared that corona virus is like HIV and we have to learn to live with it as it will not end.'[65] Ragpickers who are already engaged with such high unexpected risks are now more exposed to be getting infected by corona virus. The symptoms of getting infected by virus are much similar to what the ragpickers usually face and often ignore, which can cause seriously effect to the health of ragpickers.[66]

---

[64] Chaitanya Mallapur, Sanitation workers are at risk from Coronavirus medical waste that are not discarded properly, (July 18,2020, 02:34 PM), https://www.firstpost.com/author/indiaspend,

[65] First Post, COVID-19 could become endemic like HIV and may never go away: WHO expert Mike Ryan (June 18,2020, 03:04 PM), https://www.firstpost.com/health/covid-19-could-become-endemic-like-hiv-and-may-never-go-away-who-expert-mike-ryan-8366961.html,

[66] WHO,Coronavirus disease (COVID-19) advice for the public (June 18,2020, 02:04 PM)https://www.who.int/emergencies/diseases/novel-coronavirus-2019/advice-for-public,

2.4 IMPORTANCE OF RAGPICKERS IN INDIAN ECONOMY

Recycling is defined as a means of transforming segregated non-biodegradable waste into raw materials for producing new products and is an Indian strategy to treat the solid waste.[67] It has economic, social and environmental benefits and leads to the effective reuse of earth's finite resources, leads to a more sanitary environment, better health outcomes and inculcates civic responsibility in citizens.[68]

Indian economy is divided into 2 sectors formal and informal. The ragpickers are the part of the informal sector of the Indian economy. They do the work which is actually to be done by the civic bodies i.e. municipality. The municipality setups the dustbin, collect the waste from there and transfer it to the landfills. The essential garbage which can be recycled is segregated from such wastes and then such recyclable garbage goes for recycling. Such segregation and collection work is done by the ragpickers.[69] By doing this work, ragpickers clean up a major portion of the waste generated actually in India i.e. 62 million tonnes.[70] It is

---

[67] Solid Waste Management Rules, 2016,

[68] Deutsche Gesellschaft für, Internationale Zusammenarbeit (GIZ) GmbH Postfach 518065726 , Eschborn/Germany, Recovering resources, creating opportunities Integrating the informal sector into solid waste management ;By Silvio Ruiz, Coordinator of the Recyclers 'Association ARB (Asociación de Recicladores de Bogotá)

[69] Supra Note 31, Rajanya Bose & Anirban Bhattacharya

[70] Tara Mc Closkey, Shantha Parthan, Sameer Prasad, MALNUTRITION IN

estimated that nearly 50 lakhs Indians earned their livelihood as waste pickers in the country, after excluding those working in the recycling industry.[71] This estimate was calculated in 2002 and there is no exact figure at the current stage because the informal sector and the recycling industry in India, in general, is not a part of adequate empirical studies. Therefore, it is difficult to accurately estimate the number of waste pickers in India.

Ragpickers play an important role in the recycling value chain as they are the primary providers of raw material to the industry.[72] Ragpickers collect recyclable wastes from households, industrial buildings, and dump yards. They then clean, segregate, and sell the waste to junkyard dealers who further segregate it and sell it to the wholesalers who then sell it to recycling industries.[73]

By doing so, the ragpickers reduce the cost of the municipality and the industries. Ragpickers handle a significant portion of the waste and also protect the environment by doing

---

RAG-PICKER COMMUNITIES , XVI Annual Conference Proceedings January, 2015 ISBN no. 978-81-923211-7-2

[71] PRS India, Second National Labour Commission Report,(June 22,2020, 09:03 PM), <http://www.prsindia.org/uploads/media/Unorganised%20Sectorbill150_20071205150_National_Commission_on_Labour_2_Chapter_7_unorganised_sector_Part_A.pdf> ,

[72] Sonia Maria Dias and Melanie Samson, 'Informal Economy Monitoring Study Sector Report: Waste Pickers '(2016),(June 24,2020, 04:04 PM), http://www.wiego.org/sites/default/files/publications/files/Dias-Samson-IEMS-Waste-Picker-Sector-Report.pdf.

[73] Swachcoop, Report of the High Power Committee, (June 22,2020, 02:03 PM) http://swachcoop.com/pdf Bajaj%20Committee%20Report%201995.pdf,

their work. Ragpickers also add at least 70% value to the plastic and save the municipality a significant amount of money.[74]

Waste pickers directly contribute to the Indian economy by reducing solid waste management costs as well as environmental costs.

For example,

A study commissioned by the International Labour Organisation in 2000-2001 found that "scrap collectors collectively salvaged 144 tons of recyclable scrap before its transportation, thereby saving the Pune and Pimpri Chinchwad Municipal Corporations about Rs 16 million per annum in transportation costs alone. By implication, each waste picker contributed Rs 246 worth of unpaid labour per month to the municipality. The study also found that the annual contribution of the scrap trade to the total income generated in Pune was about Rs 185 million. [75] [76] It is estimated that in Pune alone, nearly 118,000 tonnes of material was recovered by the informal sector annually, diverting 22 percent of the recyclables away from landfills in 2006." [77] [78]

---

[74] SWACHHATA SANDESH A monthly newsletter of the Ministry of Housing and Urban Affairs (MoHUA), Government of India ,May 2018 • Volume 1 • Issue 11

[75] Poornima Chikarmane and Laxmi Narayan Organising the Unorganised: A Case Study of the KagadKach Patra Kashtakari Panchayat (Trade Union of Waste-pickers)

[76] Chikarmane, Deshpande, Narayan, 2001

[77] Poornima Chikarmane,Integrating Waste Pickers into Municipal Solid Waste Management in Pune, India,WEIGO POLICY BRIEF

[78] Ibid

Further, it was vital and difficult to quantify environmental benefits derived from the reduction of load on the landfills and the reduction of stress on our natural resource base by the recycling of paper, plastic, glass, metal, etc. This quantification of the contribution of waste pickers in Pune firmly established the role of the waste picker in the city's economy.[79]

The informal sector engages twice as many workers as the formal sector, 63 percent of the workers are fully dependent upon it for their livelihoods. Women workers in the informal sector are 10 times more than informal sector. The average earnings in the informal sector exceed the statutory minimum wage. The workers in the informal sector are recognised and are also given certain benefits, but they are sufficient for them or not always are the question.[80]

"One tonne of recycled paper saves approximately 17 trees, 2.5 barrels of oil, 4,100 Kilowatt-hours of electricity, 4 cubic meters of the landfill, and 31,780 liters of water. The share of waste paper as a raw material in India climbed from 7 percent in 1970 to 47 percent in 2011. Due to a raw material shortage, Indian paper mills are using waste paper as the raw material for the

---

[79] Supra Note 27, Ujwala Samarth

[80] Chikarmane, P., Narayan L. Study of the Economic Aspects of the Waste Informal Sector in Pune, KagadKach Patra Kashatakari Panchayat under contract to WASTE/Skat, GTZ, 2006.

manufacture of newsprint, as well as that for craft paper, used by the packaging industry. Paper and paperboard demand in India is growing at 7.8 percent per annum.[81] Of India's 500 paper mills, 241 use waste paper in the production process. The western region where Pune is located supplies 40 percent of the waste paper to manufacturing plants. Thus the efforts of waste pickers are vital to this industry."[82]

A study conducted by Women in Informal Employment: Globalising and Organising (WEIGO) in Delhi in 2016 indicated that over seventy-six percent of the waste pickers interviewed, sold the waste harvested by them to formal buyers. The informal sector is therefore also a vital link to the formal recycling industry in India. Examples of the efficiency of India's waste pickers is illustrated by the fact that every year over two fifty-nine thousand metric tons of waste paper, as well as ninety percent of Polyethylene Terephthalate (PET) bottles produced in the country, are effectively recycled, mainly due to the immense efforts of its waste pickers.[83]

---

[81] Ibid

[82] Poornima Chikarmane ,Informal Economy Monitoring Study: Waste Pickers in Pune, India

[83] Badri Chaterjee, Hindustan times, India recycles 90% of its PET waste, outperforms Japan, Europe and US: Study, Feb 19,2017 21:37 IST (June 25,2020, 06:32 PM)https://www.hindustantimes.com/mumbai-news/india-recycles-90-of-its-pet-waste-outperforms-japan-europe-and-us-study/story-yqphS1w2GdlwMYPgPtyb2L.html,

A study was conducted by A. Chandramohan, C. Ravichandran, and V. Sivasankar in Tiruchippali city in Tamil Nadu.[84] 'The study was conducted on the 65 ragpickers in the city where they found out that, all 65 rag pickers collected a total of about 882 kg of recyclable solid wastes per day in Tiruchirappalli city. On average, each rag-picker removes 13.6 kg day of waste, and on average Tiruchirappalli, generated 380 tonnes of solid waste per day, of which 34% is non-biodegradable waste including recyclable waste.' If 129 tonnes of recyclable waste is generated per day, 9500 rag-pickers would be required to clear this amount. By analysing this situation and the contribution made by ragpickers, we can understand their importance in the society.

In another the study carried out in Karnataka, Bangalore it was found out that as per 2016-2017 data, Karnataka has a population of 6.11 crore persons who on average generate 8842 metric tons of municipal solid waste per day (TPD), out of which only 7716 TPD is collected. A mere 3584 TPD treated and the remaining 3,946 TDP is sent to the 207 operational landfills present in the state.[85] 'Coming to Bengaluru, the responsibility for solid waste management in the city rests with the BBMP. The city alone produces between 3,500 to 5000 TPD and is divided into 198

---

[84] A. Chandramohan, C. Ravichandran and V. Sivasankar, Solid waste, its health impairments and role of rag pickers in Tiruchirappalli city, Tamil Nadu, Southern India
[85] http://kspcb.kar.nic.in/Annual_Report_Eng_15-16.pdf (June 25,2020, 05:06 PM)

wards to facilitate its effective governance. The population density of Bengaluru has risen by 47% in the last decade alone and this has predictably led to a massive increase in the amount of waste generated in the city.[86] It is estimated that over 15,000 waste pickers operate in Bengaluru alone.'[87]

The above-mentioned studies show the importance of ragpickers in treating the wastes in the respective cities under which the studies are carried out, but the cities under which they are carried out are some of the major cities in India. These cities play an important role in the Indian economy and so does the informal sector working in the respective cities. The ragpickers play an important role to clear the significant amount of the waste from the cities to sell it to the recycling units where the ragpickers get their livelihood and industries their raw materials, not only this but also it reduces the cost of municipalities to treat the waste and to invest more labour force. The ragpickers play an important role in the respective municipalities and the local economy and indirectly the Indian economy.

---

[86] Chandran Informal Waste Workers Contribution in Bangalore,(June 25,2020, 08:20 PM) https://hasirudala.in/wp-content/uploads/2016/08/1.-Full-Paper-pdf
[87] https://www.hasirudala.in/wpcontent/uploads/2016/08/Lodha_Siddhartha_PApaper.pdf, (June 25,2020, 11:06 PM)

CHAPTER 3

RAG PICKERS AND THE CRITICAL ANALYSIS OF THE SOCIAL SECURITY SCHEME EMPHASISING HEALTH INSURANCE

3.1 INSURANCE

In India, insurance is provided as the social security benefit to the beneficiaries. 'Insurance has a deep-rooted history in India as it has been mentioned in the writings of Manu (Manusmriti), Yagnavalkya (Dharmasastra), and Kautilya (Arthasastra).'[88] It talks in terms of accumulating the resources that could be re-distributed in times of calamities like fire, flood, epidemics, or famine. In ancient India, there are traces of insurance in the form of marine trade loans and carriers contracts. With the passage of time it got developed and evolved by withdrawing and adopting the policies of other countries, especially England.

The insurance sector is divided into two categories: general insurance and life insurance. The life insurance policy can be withdrawn on the event of death or the maturity of the policy and the general insurance policy will pay for the losses that may occur during the policy period only. The general insurance policies

---

[88] IRDAI, About, (July 01,2020, 01:08 PM) https://www.irdai.gov.in/ADMINCMS/cms/NormalData_Layout.aspx?page=PageNo4&mid=2,

include health insurance, travel insurance, motor insurance, marine insurance, home insurance, commercial insurance and digit insurance which include and offer insurance policies for mobile, bicycle, shop protection, and others.[89]

3.1.a LIFE INSURANCE

In 1818, the life insurance business was started in India and the Oriental Life Insurance Company in Calcutta was established. It failed and in 1870 the British Insurance Act was enacted and the Bombay Mutual (1871), Oriental (1874), and the Empire of India (1897) were started in the Bombay residency. With this, the foreign insurance companies dominated the Indian insurance companies and did good business in India.[90]

'The Indian Life Assurance Companies 'Act in 1912 was the first statutory measure to regulate life business in India.'[91] In 1938, with a view to protect the interest of the public, the earlier legislation was amended and consolidated and the Insurance Act 1938 was formed for effective control over the activities of insurers. The amendments were made from time to time, and as the amendment Act of 1950 abolished the principal agencies there were a lot of insurance companies and the competition was high which raised the allegations of unfair trade practices. Therefore,

---

[89] Godgit, All about General Insurances (July. 02,2020, 08:09 PM)https://www.godigit.com/guides/types-of-general-insurance;
[90] Supra Note 1
[91] R.N.Chaudhary, General Principles of Law of Insurance.

the government of India decided to nationalise insurance business and an ordinance was issued on 19th January 1956, nationalising the life insurance sector. The Life Insurance Corporation came into existence in the same year.[92] The LIC absorbed 154 Indian, 16 non-Indian insurers as also 75 provident societies—245 Indian and foreign insurers in all. The LIC had a monopoly till the late 90s when the insurance sector was reopened to the private sector.[93]

3.1.b. GENERAL INSURANCE

The history of general insurance dates back to the industrial revolution in the western region and the trade and commerce in the 17th century. It came to India with the Britishers with the establishment of a Triton Insurance Company Ltd in the year 1850 in Calcutta. In 1907, the Indian Mercantile Insurance Ltd was set up which was the first company to carry out all types of general insurances. In 1957 general insurance council was formed which was a wing of the insurance association in India which framed a code of conduct for ensuring fair conduct and sound business practices.[94]

In 1968, the Insurance Act was amended to regulate the investment and set the minimum solvency margins. "In 1972 the

---

[92] Ibid
[93] IRDAI, About, (July 01,2020, 01:08 PM) https://www.irdai.gov.in/ADMINCMS/cms/NormalData_Layout.aspx?page=PageNo4&mid=2,
[94] Ibef, Insurance Sector,(Nov 19,2019, 02:48 PM) https://www.ibef.org/industry/insurance-sector-india.aspx,

general insurance business was nationalised with the passing of the General Insurance Business Act w.e.f from 1st Jan 1973. 107 insurers were amalgamated and grouped into 4 companies namely National Insurance Company Ltd., the New India Assurance Company Ltd., the Oriental Insurance Company Ltd. and the United India Insurance Company Ltd. The General Insurance Corporation of India was incorporated as a company in 1971 and it commenced business from January 1st, 1973."[95]

3.1.c INSURANCE REGULATORY AND DEVELOPMENT AUTHORITY (IRDA)

The process of re-opening the insurance sector began in the early 1990s, by setting up a committee under the chairmanship of R.N Malhotra, former Governor of the RBI. The main purpose of setting up this committee was to propose recommendations for reforms in the insurance sector. The objective was to complement the reforms initiated in the financial sector. The report was submitted in 1994 which included many other things but it highly recommended that the private sector be permitted to enter the insurance industry. The committee also stated that foreign companies should be allowed to enter by floating Indian companies preferably a joint venture with Indian partners.[96]

---

[95] Ibid

[96] IRDAI, About, (July 01,2020, 01:08 PM) https://www.irdai.gov.in/ADMINCMS/cms/NormalData_Layout.aspx?page=PageNo4&mid=2,

Following the recommendations of the Malhotra Committee report, in 1999, the government constituted an autonomous body to regulate the insurance industry named as the Insurance Regulatory and Development Authority (IRDA). The IRDA was incorporated as a statutory body in April 2000. The key objectives of the IRDA included the promotion of competition to enhance customer satisfaction through increased consumer choice and lower premiums while ensuring the financial security of the insurance market.

The IRDA opened up the market and invited the applications for registrations in August 2000, and foreign companies were allowed ownership of up to 26%. The authority has the power to frame rules and regulations for the insurance companies under the Sec 114A of the insurance Act, 1938.[97]

Subsidiaries of the General Insurance Corporation of India were restructured in December 2000, and at the same time GIC was converted into a national re-insurer and four subsidiary companies were delinked after passing a bill in July 2002. "Today, there are 31 general insurance companies including the ECGC and Agriculture Insurance Corporation of India and 24 life insurance companies operating in the country. Today insurance services add about 7% to the country of GDP."[98]

---

[97] Ibid
[98] Ibid

3.2. SOCIAL SECURITY

Social security provides social protection to a certain class of people in the society irrespective of their employment sector. Social security refers to the protection extended by the state to its members to protect them from various contingencies of life to promote the state by making the beneficiaries more productive without having any anxiety of the future.[99]

Social security is a concept as well as a system. It represents a system of protection by the state to the individuals who need such protection. Such protections are extended by the state in any relevant contingencies such as health, retirement, death, life accident, or any other conditions that are beyond the control of the individual member of the society. The state as an agent of the society plays an important role to provide a protective cover to the poor and deprived people who are in need so that they can be more productive without having any anxiety for the security and promote the economic condition of the country.[100]

"Social security is asserted in "Article 22 of the Universal Declaration of Human Rights, states that everyone, as a member of society, has the right to social security and is entitled to realisation, through national effort and international co-operation and per the organisation and resources of each State, of the economic, social and cultural rights indispensable for his dignity and the free

---

[99] Ibid
[100] Ibid

development of his personality."[101] In simple terms, the signatories agree that the society in which a person lives should help them to develop and to make the most of all the advantages (culture, work, social welfare) which are offered to them in the country.

3.2.a SOCIAL SECURITY AND UNORGANISED SECTOR

Social security is always provided to the target population to uplift the condition of them, or to the entire citizen providing the eligibility criteria or to each citizen of the country compulsorily, to enjoy the benefits of the government schemes.[102]

Indian being signatory to the declaration offers social security to the citizens in various ways and health care is one of the protections which are offered by the government of India. The government makes different schemes like social security to the beneficiaries where each scheme had it's different beneficiaries, and the same is funded by the government. These schemes have different objectives to promote. Insurance is one of the ways to offer protection to beneficiaries in monetary terms where they can be secured and protected against any future contingency.

---

[101] United Nations Human Rights Commission, Universal Declaration of Human Rights at 70: 30 Articles on 30 Articles - Article 22, (July. 04,2020 04:48 PM) https://www.ohchr.org/EN/NewsEvents/Pages/DisplayNews.aspx?NewsID=23962&LangID=E,

[102] Report Of The Working Group On Social Security For The Tenth Five Year Plan" (2002- 2007) Government of India, Planning Commission October- 2001 (Sr.No.48/2001).

Organised sector consists of the formal labour class which is also called licensed organisations and also enjoys all other employee benefits recommended by the government.[103] The unorganised sector consists of the informal labour class and also know as unlicensed organisations or self-employed which includes handicrafts and handloom workers or rural traders or other labours which are described by ILO under the unorganised sector.[104] The workers in this sector neither have any fixed employer nor the employment benefits. The term informal sector was first used by International Labour Organisation i.e. ILO, which defined "informality as a 'way of doing things characterised by (a) easy of entry; (b) reliance of indigenous resources: (c) family ownership; (d) small scale operations; (e) labour-intensive and adaptive technology; (e) skills acquired outside of the formal sector; (g) unregulated and competitive markets."[105]

'For the first time in India, a comprehensive Social Security Scheme for the Unorganised sector was proposed by The proposal of the National Commission for Enterprises in the Unorganised Sector with the Social Security Act in 2008.' According to NCEUS unorganised sector is defined as "The unorganised sector consists

---

[103] Gender Dimensions of the Informal Sector and Informal Employment in India Page no. 2-3,Global Forum On Gender Statistics Esa/ Stat/Ac.168/41 26-28 January (Nov.22,2019. 03:45PM),
Https://Unstats.Un.Org/Unsd/Gender/Ghana_Jan2009/Doc41.Pdf, y 2009,
[104] The ILO And The Informal Sector An Institutional History, Page no. 9
[105] Supra Note 91

of all unincorporated private enterprises owned by individuals or households engaged in the sale and production of goods and services operated on a proprietary or partnership basis and with less than ten total workers".[106]

"The people in the unorganised sector include –

1. Building construction workers
2. Casual labourers
3. Cobblers
4. Employees in shops and commercial establishments
5. Farmers and agriculture labourers
6. Fishermen
7. Forest workers
8. Garment makers
9. Handloom and power loom, workers,
10. Hawkers
11. Head load workers
12. Labourers employed in small scale industries
13. Manual labourers in carpentry, trade, transport, communication, etc. 18. Street vendors
14. Persons engaged in animal husbandry, fishing, horticulture, beekeeping, toddy tapping, etc.
15. Rural artisans
16. Sharecroppers
17. Small and marginal farmers

---

[106] Ibid

18. Sweepers and scavengers
19. Tin smiths
20. Workers in Bidi and cigar factories
21. Workers in matches and crackers industry
22. Workers in tanneries"[107]

'The National Commission for Enterprises in the Unorganised Sector (NCEUS) was constituted on 20.09.2004 by the United Progressive Alliance (UPA) Government when it came into power in 2004, under the chairmanship of Dr. Arjun Sengupta.' The Commission has the mandate to examine the problems of the unorganised sector and suggest measures to overcome them. Many bills were proposed and rejected before the Ministry of Labour and Employment brought out the bill, i.e., the Unorganised Sector Workers' Social Security Bill, 2007 before the Rajya Sabha during the zero hours. The Bill was not accepted in its original form and after making necessary amendments the final bill was passed as the 'Unorganised Workers Social Security Act, 2008'. This became the first social security act for the unorganised sector in India.[108]

---

[107] PRS India,National Commission On Labour 2 Chapter 7 Unorganised Sector Part A.(July.06,2020. 05:34PM)
https://www.prsindia.org/sites/default/files/bill_files/bill150_20071205150_National_Commission_on_Labour_2_Chapter_7_unorganised_sector_Part_A_1.pdf, last

[108] The Challenge of Employment in India An Informal Economy Perspective Volume I - Main Report National Commission For Enterprises In The Unorganised Sector

UNORGANISED WORKERS SOCIAL SECURITY ACT 2008

The long title of the Act provides that the Act is passed to "provide for the social security and welfare of unorganised workers and for other matters connected to therewith or incidental thereto."[109] Further, Section 3 (1) of the Act provides that the Central and the State Government shall formulate and notify schemes from time to time covering life and disability, health and maternity benefits, old age protection, and any other benefit as may be determined by the Central Government. The Act permits and guides the Centre and State government to formulate schemes for the unorganised sector.[110] To claim social security benefits under the Act, the unorganised worker needs to register himself after fulfilling certain conditions specified in Section 10 of the Act.

SOCIAL SECURITY SCHEMES UNDER THE ACT INCLUDED IN SCHEDULE I

The unorganised sector workers were considered under the various schemes, the schedule 1 of the Act describes the various social security schemes which include.

" Aam Admi Bima Yojana.

---

[109] Supra Note 107
[110] Ibid

Handicraft Artisans 'Comprehensive Welfare Scheme.

Handloom Weavers 'Comprehensive Welfare Scheme.

Indira Gandhi National Old Age Pension Scheme.

Janani Suraksha Yojana.

Janshree Bima Yojana.

National Family Benefit Scheme.

National Scheme for Welfare of Fishermen.

Pension to Master craft persons.

Rashtriya Swasthya Bima Yojana."[111]

These social security schemes are formulated under the act to provide benefits to the unorganised sector.

3.2.c SOCIAL SECURITY FOR RAGPICKERS AND NEED OF IT

Ragpickers are the workers under the unorganised sector which constitutes a major part of the economy and plays an important role in the Indian economy. The unorganised sector constitutes more than 90 percent of the total workforce in the country and about 50 percent of the national product is accounted

---

[111] Id

for by the Unorganised Sector. Ragpickers mostly do the work which is done by the civic bodies which are to collect the garbage or to segregate the wastes or to segregate the recyclable garbage.[112] By this work, ragpickers clean up a major portion of the waste generated actually in India i.e. 62 million tonnes.[113] It is estimated that nearly 50 lakhs Indians earned their livelihood as waste pickers in the country, even excluding those working in the recycling industry.[114] This estimate was calculated in 2002 and there is no exact figure at the current stage because the informal sector and the recycling industry in India, in general, is not been part of adequate empirical studies. So it is difficult to accurately estimate the number of waste pickers in India. But sadly ragpickers are a very socially and economically deprived class of the society. Ragpickers play an important role in the recycling value chain as they are the primary providers of raw material to the industry.[115] Ragpickers collect recyclable wastes from households, industrial buildings, and dump yards. They then clean, segregate, and sell the waste to junkyard dealers who further segregate it and sell it to the wholesalers who then sell it to recycling industries.[116] By doing so, the ragpickers significantly reduce the cost of the municipality and the industries. Ragpickers handle a significant portion of the waste

---

[112] Supra Note 31, Rajanya Bose & Anirban Bhattacharya
[113] Supra Note 70, Tara Mc Closkey, Shantha Parthan, Sameer Prasad
[114] Supra Note 107, PRS India
[115] Supra Note 72, Sonia Maria Dias and Melanie Samson
[116] Swachcoop, Report of the High Power Committee,(June.12,2020. 07:32 PM) http://swachcoop.com/pdf Bajaj%20Committee%20Report%201995.pdf,

and also protect the environment by doing their work. Ragpickers by doing their work add at least 70% value to the plastic and save the municipality a significant amount of money.[117]

Waste pickers directly contribute to the Indian economy by reducing solid waste management costs as well as environmental costs. In doing so, they come across many health hazards and other occupational hazards which mostly affect their health. The rag pickers often work alone and for long hours without having any protective gear that can protect them from any injury which is caused by the broken glasses or sharp objects or any other necessary equipment which are helpful to segregate the garbage or to disassemble the products which they find. They often inhale the harmful gases on the dumpsites and often get bitten by various insects or animals which poison the body.[118]

3.3. SOCIAL SECURITY SCHEMES FOR THE RAGPICKERS:-

---

[117] SWACHHATA SANDESH A monthly newsletter of the Ministry of Housing and Urban Affairs (MoHUA), Government of India ,May 2018 • Volume 1 • Issue 11

[118] International Labour Organization International Programme On The Elimination Of Child Labour (Ipec) Investigating The Worst Forms Of Child Labour No. 4 Nepal situation Of Child Ragpickers: AA Rapid Assessment, Page no. 9

Recognising the importance of rag picking and the ragpicker's government has formulated various social security schemes for them that are given as under Insurance schemes:

1. PRADHAN MANTRI JAN AROGYA YOJANA (PMJAY)

Pradhan Mantri Jan Arogya Yojna is also popularly known as PM-JAY. "It was launched by the Hon'ble prime minister of India, Shri Narendra Modi on 23rd September 2018. This is the largest health assurance scheme in the world which aims at providing a health cover of Rs 5 lakhs per year which includes secondary and tertiary care hospitalisation to over 10.74 crore poor and vulnerable families. The beneficiaries which are included in the scheme are based on the deprivation and occupational criteria of socio-economic care census 2011 for rural and urban areas respectively. PM-JAY was earlier also known as the National Health Protection Scheme (NHPS) before being rechristened. It also subsumes the then-existing Rashtriya Swasthya Bima Yojana (RSBY) scheme which was launched in 2008. The PM-JAY also includes the families that are covered by RSBY and also include the other families which are present in the SECC2011 database. PM-JAY is fully funded by the Government and cost is shared between the Centre and State Government respectively."[119]

---

[119] PMJAY, About, (July 07,2020. 04:08 PM) https://pmjay.gov.in/about/pmjay

KEY FEATURES OF PM-JAY

- This is the largest health insurance scheme in the word which is fully financed by the Government.
- It provides a cover-up to Rs. 5 lakhs per family per year.
- It covers secondary and tertiary care hospitalisation across public and private empanelled hospitals in India.
- Covers 10.74 crore poor and vulnerable families which are eligible for the benefits.
- Provides cashless access to health care.
- The scheme also covers the pre and post hospitalisation expenses. (3days pre hospitalisation and 15 days post hospitalisation)
- No restriction on age, gender, or family size.
- Also covers pre-existing diseases."[120]

DRAWBACKS: State should choose to implement the scheme or not. The SECC data also includes those persons who do not come in BPL now or those who do not need the free health insurance benefits. The scheme has a lot of terms and conditions for availing the benefits. If a person can avail the benefits in one category, he can get rejected because of falling in other conditions.

2. RASHTRIYA SWASTHYA BIMA YOJANA (RSBY)

---

[120] Ibid

In 2008 RSBY was introduced by the Ministry of labour and Employment for unorganised workers in the country. The main object was to provide families that are below the poverty line to provide the best health care service and social security which was also later expanded to unorganised workers who are marginally above the poverty line. The scheme is allowed to get the best medical facilities in health hazards regarding old age, maternity, disability, and General ailments.[121]

HIGHLIGHTED FEATURES OF RASHTRIYA SWASTHYA BIMA YOJANA

"
- Unorganised workers are eligible to get hospitalisation expense coverage up to Rs. 30,000.
- Premium charges are directly paid by the central and state government respectively.
- No age limit provided for coverage under the scheme.
- The beneficiaries to avail the benefits should pay 30rs as registration fees.
- Pre-existing diseases are also covered under the scheme.
- The schemes cover the entire family and provide complete medical coverage to everyone in the family.

---

[121] PolicyX, RSBY, (July,03,2020. 01:02 AM) https://www.policyx.com/health-insurance/articles/rashtriya-swasthya-bima-yojana-rsby/ ,

- The RSBY scheme provides incentives for the stakeholders which imply that the insurer gets incentives from the Government for the number of members enrolled.
- A smart card is provided to each insured family.
- The scheme is made using a data management system that is responsible for tracking.
- Transactions across the country and sending reports periodically.
- The scheme covers up to 5 members in the family.
- 1000 Rs. Maximum Transportation charges are included; Up to Rs 100 per visit is included in the coverage."[122]

DRAWBACKS:- State should choose to implement the scheme or not. The eligible beneficiary has to draw a card from the officials which sometimes become a hectic procedure.

3. RAJIV GANDHI JEEVAN DAYEE AROGYA YOJANA, NOW CALLED THE MAHATMA JYOTIBA PHULE JEEVAN DAYEE AROGYA YOJANA (MJPJAY)

Rajiv Gandhi Jeevandayee Arogya Yojana (RGJAY) has been implemented throughout the state of Maharashtra in a phased

---

[122] RSBY, About (June 12,2020 12:34AM) http://www.rsby.gov.in/how_works.html.

manner for 4 years. State Government rechristened it to the Mahatma Jyotiba Phule Jan Arogya Yojana (MJPJAY) resolution issued on 13th April 2017. 'Its main object is to improve access of Below Poverty Line (BPL) and Above Poverty Line (APL) families (excluding White Card Holders as defined by Civil Supplies Department) to quality medical care for identified speciality services requiring hospitalisation for surgeries and therapies or consultations through an identified Network of health care providers.'

The scheme is available for all the eligible beneficiaries of Maharashtra state i.e. it is applicable all the 36 districts in Maharashtra. The scheme is for all the eligible families who are holding Yellow Ration Card, Antyodaya Anna Yojana Card (AAY), Annapurna Card and Orange Ration Card along with Farmers from 14 agriculturally distressed districts of Maharashtra. The qualification for the farmers will be based on the white ration card and 7/12extract or certified from the concerned Talathi. And in case of family the coverage applies only to those whose names are listed on the valid Orange/Yellow Ration Card. The scheme covers all pre existing diseases and provides coverage of up to Rs 1,50,000/- per family per year in any empanelled hospital. And In case of renal transplant surgery, the immunosuppressive therapy is required for a period of 1 year. So the upper ceiling for Renal Transplant would be Rs. 2,50,000 per operation as an exceptional package exclusively for this procedure.[123]

SALIENT FEATURES OF MJPJAY

"
- The insurance coverage and premium is borne by the Government of Maharashtra.
- Covers up to Rs 1,50,000 per family per year.
- Covers surgeries, diagnostics, medications and follow-up consultations and treatment.
- All pre-existing diseases are covered.
- Government empanelled hospitals and also several private hospitals are included.
- Also provides access to health camps conducted at government empanelled hospitals."[124]

DRAWBACKS: - Only tertiary care is being covered, often patient incur out of pocket expenses.

4. TRUST HOSPITALS

---

[123] MJPJAY, About, (June 02,2020, 02:56 PM)https://www.jeevandayee.gov.in/MJPJAY/FrontServlet?RequestType=CommonRH&actionVal=RightFrame&pageundefined%3E%3E%3Cb%3EMJPJAY%3C/ b%3E&pageName=MJPJAY&mainMenu=About&subMenu=MJPJAY.
[124] ACKO, Health Insurance (June 02,2020, 04:42 PM)https://www.acko.com/health-insurance/.

Trust Hospitals scheme is only for Maharashtra state, the hospitals which are registered under the Bombay Public Trust Act, 1950 are required to reserve 10 percent of their beds for Below the Poverty Line (BPL)/ Economically Weaker Section (EWS) patients; they are also required to have an Indigent Patient Fund (IPF), constituting 2 percent of their annual turnover, and to use this fund to provide free treatment to BPL patients and 50 percent concession to EWS patients.

Trust Hospitals which are registered under the Bombay Public Trust Act 1950 get many concessions since they are expected to provide emergency services to all and quality medical services to economically weaker sections at free or at concessional rates. Under Section 41AA of the Bombay Public Trust Act, 1950, the scheme for treatment to indigent patients and weaker section patients was approved by the Hon. Bombay High Court on the 14th of October 2005. The scheme came into effect from the 1st of September 2006.[125]

THE SALIENT FEATURES OF THE SCHEME ARE-

- All trust hospitals " shall be under a legal obligation to reserve and earmark 10% of the total number of operational beds for indigent patients and provide medical treatment to the indigent patients free of cost and reserve and earmark

---

[125] KKPKP, Charitable Trust Hospitals ,(June 04,2020. 03:34 PM)http://www.kkpkp-pune.org/charitable-trust-hospitals.html.

- 10% of the total number of operational beds at concessional rate to the weaker section patients."
- The trust hospital should have an annual turnover above Rs. 5 lakhs.
- 2% of gross billing of all patients other than patients treated under this scheme should be assigned to a separate fund called the Indigent Patients Fund (IPF).and if any shortfall is faced then it should be adjusted in subsequent months.
- Certain services should be provided free to indigent patients such as bed, RMO services, nursing care, food, linen, water, electricity, housekeeping, and routine diagnostics.
- The charges should be as per the lowest class.
- Information should be provided to the office of the charity commissioner regarding the amount collected in the IPF and profiles of the patients treated under the scheme.

The economic status of the patients should be scrutinised by the medical or social worker using any one of the documents- i) certificate of income from the Tahasildar ii) ration card/ BPL card.[126]

DRAWBACKS: - Hospitals sometimes do not display the number of free beds, and often fake the data or often refuse the treatment by giving some reasons or shifts patients to other hospitals where bed may be available.

---

[126] Ibid

5. JAN AROGYA POLICY

KagadKach Patra Kashtakari Panchayat (KKPKP) is the holder of this policy, the policy is provided by the New India Assurance Company (NIA) since January 2003. The premium for the policy is paid by the Pune Municipal Corporation from its annual budget. This is a medical insurance policy offered to those who are economically backward. The insured can receive an amount of Rs.5, 000 and claim tax benefits of up to Rs.10, 000 under Section 80D of the Income Tax Act, 1961. The policy covers the family members as well as the individuals. Under the Jan Arogya Bima Policy, there is no facility for medical checkups. Also, the benefit of cumulative bonus is not offered under this policy. [127] [128]

Highlighted features of Jan Arogya Bima Policy are listed below:
- sum assured is Rs 5000 per annum per member
- Minimum age eligibility is 18-70 years
- medical checkup is not required
- Treatment admissible in registered private and public hospitals.
- Policy covers hospitalisation and not out-patient care.[129]

---

[127] Bank Bazaar, Life Insurances, Jan arogya Bima Policy, (June 04,2020. 05:34 PM)https://www.bankbazaar.com/life-insurance/jan-arogya-bima-policy.html .
[128] IRDAI, Jan Arogya Bima Policy, (June 04,2020. 06:34 PM) https://www.irdai.gov.in/ADMINCMS/cms/Uploadedfiles/NEWINDIA15/Jan%20Arogya%20Bima%20Policy.pdf.

DRAWBACKS: - Medical checkup benefits are not included in the scheme. Outpatient procedures are not covered. Pregnancy and childbirth expenses are not covered under the scheme.

6. SHAHARI GAREEB VAIDYAKEEYA SAHAYYA YOJANA (URBAN POOR HEALTH SCHEME)

Citizens living in the jurisdiction of Pune Municipal Corporation can avail of the benefits from this scheme, especially waste-pickers (special inclusion) through a General Body Resolution in February 2015. It covers the ragpicker's immediate family members. The solid waste management department of Pune Municipal Corporation pays 200 Rs /- which is a total amount of membership registration fees for the Members of KKPKP. The scheme covers the hospital expenditure up to one lakhs rupees where the bill is to be shared in 9:1 ration i.e. 90 % of the bill is shared by the PMC and 10 % is to be paid by the patient.[130]

DRAWBACKS: - The schemes are only limited to the empanelled hospitals, mostly public hospitals where a yellow ration card will get free treatment. The applicant's name should be on the ration card.

3.3. RELEVANT EDUCATION SCHEMES FOR CHILDREN OF RAGPICKERS

---

[129] Supra Note 27, Ujwala Samarth
[130] Pune Municipality (June 12,2020. 05:24 PM)https://pmc.gov.in/pmc-web,

1. RIGHT TO EDUCATION

"The Constitution (Eighty-sixth Amendment) Act, 2002 inserted Article 21-A in the Constitution of India to provide free and compulsory education of all children in the age group of six to fourteen years as a Fundamental Right in such a manner as the State may, by law, determine. The Right of Children to Free and Compulsory Education (RTE) Act, 2009, which represents the consequential legislation envisaged under Article 21-A, means that every child has a right to full-time elementary education of satisfactory and equitable quality in a formal school which satisfies certain essential norms and standards. Following this, the government has framed that there should be 25% reserved seats in private (non-government-funded) schools to backward caste and economically backward classes and children with disabilities which also includes the child ragpickers or the children of them."[131]

2. SCHOLARSHIPS FOR CHILDREN OF PARENTS WORKING IN UNCLEAN OCCUPATIONS

"Pre-Matric Scholarships to the Children of those engaged in occupations involving cleaning and prone to health hazards. The Government of India is implementing this Scheme since 1977-78. For those children who are engaged in the occupation involving

---

[131] Right to Education, About (June 06,2020. 01:38 PM) http://righttoeducation.in/know-your-rte/about

cleaning and occupations which are prone to health hazards, 100 % Central assistance is provided to State from the centre for expenditure as well as for implementing the schemes." The objective of the scheme includes waste pickers as one of the beneficiaries of the scheme. The scholarship is given to only those children who are studying from class 1 to class 10th. "The beneficiaries are entitled to get a scholarship of in the case of Day Scholars, Class I to X Rs. 225/- p.m. for ten months and Hostellers: Class III to X Rs. 700/- p.m. for ten months and besides an ad-hoc grant of Rs. 750/- per student per annum, and Rs. 1000/- per student per annum to hostellers would be admissible. Besides this, there are additional provisions of allowances for students amongst target groups with disabilities."[132] [133]

3.3. SOCIAL WELFARE SCHEMES FOR RAGPICKERS

1. ATAL PENSION YOJANA

This pension scheme was launched by the Prime Minister for the unorganised sector in 2015. The beneficiary amount differs from

---

[132] Ibid

[133] Social Justice, Scheme List, (June 15,2020. 04:14 PM) http://socialjustice.nic.in/SchemeList/Send/24?mid=24541

the variable and based on individual choice. The scheme also calculates the number of years or amount of contribution which determines the pension amount. The eligible beneficiaries are aged from 18 years of age to 40 years of age. The central government contributes 50% of the amount deposited by beneficiary but is capped at Rs. 1,000/annum.[134]

2. **SANJAY GANDHI NIRADHAR YOJANA**

"This scheme applies to destitute persons of the age below 65 years, orphan children, all types of handicapped, a person suffering from a critical illness like T. B. cancer, AIDS and leprosy. It also destitute windows including those of farmers who committed suicide, destitute divorced women and women in process of divorce, women freed from prostitution and outraged women. The beneficiaries are entitled to get Rs. 600 per month. This amount is given to a single beneficiary and Rs. 900 per month if there are two or more beneficiaries in the family. The eligibility age is up to 65 years and annual family income should be under Rs. 21,000 per annum." [135]

3. **JANASHREE BIMA YOJANA (JBY) NOW CALLED AAM ADMI BIMA YOJANA**

---

[134] Bank of Baroda, Atal Pension Yojna, (June 15,2020. 05:24 PM) https://www.bankofbaroda.in/atal-pension-yojna.htm.
[135] Sanjay Gandhi Yojana, Pune, (June 15,2020. 06:14 PM) ,https://pune.gov.in/scheme/sanjay-gandhi-yojana/.

Life Insurance Coverage limit: Rs. 30,000 for natural death, Rs. 75,000 for accidental death, and Rs. 37,500 for partial handicap. The benefits go to nominee mentioned in the insurance application. The scheme is available for urban poor, who are in the age of 18-59 years and the cost of scheme is of Rs. 200 which is shared between state and centre.[136]

Indian economy consists of more than 90 % of unorganised sector, recognising raw importance of the unorganised sector government have created and has taken many initiatives to protect the unorganised sector and ragpickers in it. The above-mentioned scheme shows that the government is trying to offer protection in each way possible be it health or life or employment or education, the government is trying to offer their helping hand to the unorganised sector since 2008 i.e. by creating the social security Act for Unorganised Sector 2008. Since then the government is trying to offer their helping hand and to take more n more initiative for the backbone of our Indian economy. The eligible beneficiaries should enjoy the benefits which are provided to them and should spread the word about such schemes so that the unorganised sector can get aware of such schemes. Sometimes there may be loopholes in the schemes, but such loopholes must not prevent the eligible beneficiaries from availing the benefits. Unorganised sector should be made aware about such schemes and steps should be taken to

---

[136] Acko, Health Insurance, Aam Admi Bima Yojana , (June 16,2020. 01:45 PM) https://www.acko.com/health-insurance/aam-aadmi-bima-yojana/.

improve the schemes and such schemes should be utilised by the eligible beneficiaries.

3.4. JUDICIAL GUIDELINES

3.4.A. MUNICIPAL COUNCIL - RATLAM VS. VARDHICHAND [137]

"The case is mainly focuses on the Ratlam municipality who failed to provide the sanitation facility to the general public on the grounds of insufficient funds which municipality had. The Supreme Court held municipality responsible and stated that municipality cannot run away from its duty by pleading financial inability and was ordered to take immediate actions to provide sanitation facilities and services.

This decision rejected the municipalities 'defence that it lacked the funds, nothing that the relevant Indian law obligates the municipality to fulfil its public health duties. Here we can see that general public refers to the slum dwellers or the public who don't have private sanitation facility. The lack of facilities lands them in contaminating the streets or other area feasible, which can be unhygienic. Here we can see the judicial presiding for all the

---

[137] Municipal Council, Ratlam v. Shri Vardhichand & Others, 1980 AIR 1622, 1981 SCR (1) 97

municipalities to provide proper sanitation facilities to the general public." [138]

3.4.B. DR. B.L. WADEHRA V. UNION OF INDIA [139]

"This is a landmark case which dealt with the right to clean environment of the citizens and obligatory duty of the government to keep the city clean. The PIL filed by the petitioner resulted into holding Government liable to keep city clean and issuing guidelines to the municipalities for making strict laws for keeping the city clean. The court also held that 'non-availability of funds inadequacy or inefficiency of the staff, insufficiency of machinery etc. cannot be pleaded as ground for non-performance of their statutory obligations.' The court in this case also issued **guidelines to the municipal corporations** to start with the schemes, like Swachha Bangalore/Delhi, separation of recyclable waste/non-bio-degradable waste from other waste, and to collect domestic hazardous waste at source by means of door-to-door collection by municipal workmen or through private contractors." [140]

GUIDELINES BY THE SUPREME COURT IN THIS CASE

---

[138] Muncipal Council Ratlam v Shri Vardhichand and others, (June 20,2020. 07:40 PM) https://www.escr-net.org/caselaw/2019/municipal-council-ratlam-v-shri-vardhichand-others-1980-air-1622-1981-scr-1-97.

[139] Dr.B.L.Wadehra vs. Union Of India & Ors , 1996 SCC (2) 594, JT 1996 (3) 38

[140] Solid Waste Management An Indian Legal Profile, (July 05,2020. 01:24 PM) https://nlsenlaw.org/solid-waste-management-an-indian-legal-profile/.

- "The Court issued various directives to MCD and NMCD regarding the collection, transportation and disposal of garbage and hospital waste.
- To install sufficient number of incinerators particularly in the hospitals with 50 beds or more.
- Sanitary Land Fill (SLF) were to be identified for disposal of garbage and solid waste.
- MCD and NMCD with NEERI were also directed to find out alternate method/methods of garbage and solid waste disposal.
- Supreme Court also mentioned that the residents of Delhi must be educated through mass media regarding their civic duties and that in case they violate any provision of the respective Acts they must be penalised.
- Directions were also issued in the matter of collecting and disposal of garbage.
- The Government was directed to appoint Municipal Magistrate for the trial of the erring persons. And the Central Pollution Board and Delhi Pollution Committee were also directed to send inspection teams to ascertain that collection transportation and disposal of garbage/waste is carried out satisfactorily.
- The Court, through this decision also tried to evolve a code of conduct for the municipal authorities and general public to collect, and dispose of the garbage/solid waste."[141]

---

[141] Ibid

3.4.C. PEOPLE FOR TRANSPARENCY VS STATE OF PUNJAB [142]

In this case, the state of Punjab for the first time tried to initiate the Municipal solid waste management plan in the Bhatinda District, where the government has accorded Environmental Clearance for establishment of Integrated Municipal Solid Waste Management facility in an area of 20 acre at Mansa road, Bhatinda and establishment of Engineered Sanitary Land Fill facility in an area of 36.8 acres in the Revenue Estate of Village Mandi Khurd, District Bhatinda to Municipal Corporation. This was opposed by the public on the environmental grounds, but the tribunal allowed the government to setup the plant there and asked the government to explain the model plan to the petitioners. The plan included that the collection of wastes can be done by the Municipal workers themselves, or can be done by contracting the collection of wastes to a competent organisation, or privatising the work through ragpickers and *kabaris* or any suitable agencies. This was the first case where MSW management plan was started by the state of Punjab which allowed waste pickers ragpickers or *kabaris* to collect the wastes.[143]

---

[142] People for Transparency through Kamal Anand vs. State of Punjab & Ors; Original Application No. 40(THC) of 2013

[143] People for Transparency through kamal anand vs State of Punjab (July 13,2020. 04:04 AM) ,https://www.wwfindia.org/?13287/People-for-Transparency-Through-Kamal-Anand--Vs--State-of-Punjab-Ors.

3.5. EXECUTIVE GUIDELINES ON INDIA'S RAG PICKERS

There is no parliamentary legislation on the ragpickers, but there are some rules or committee recommendations that were constituted to look into improving efficiency of SWM in India which also provides some guideline on improving the lives of Rag pickers in India.

3.5.A. REPORT OF THE J.S BAJAJ HIGH POWER COMMITTEE, 1994

This was the first committee which recognised the importance of Rag pickers in managing the solid waste in India. The committee was constituted after the outbreak of Surat plague in 1994. The committee had many practical recommendations which were related to the waste segregation or setting up the collection units, or providing the appropriate equipments and vehicles for transportation of waste. The committee recognised the importance of ragpickers and clearly pointed out the health hazards the ragpickers faced and the importance of ragpickers. The committee recommended for setting up the community toilets for improving ragpickers hygiene. The committee also recommended for capacity building programs and establishing NGO or association for ragpickers. It also suggested that the ragpickers should be given employment by local municipalities to avoid the middlemen. [144] [145]

3.5.B. THE ASIM BURMAN COMMITTEE, 1999

As solid waste management practice was failing resulting into the problems of sanitation, health and environmental degradation. PIL was filed in The Hon'ble Supreme Court of India by **Mrs. Almitra H Patel & another vs. Union of India & others,**[146] seeking directions from the Hon'ble Supreme Court of India to the Government for improving Solid Waste Management practices efficiently. During the hearing of the case SC constituted a committee for suggesting improvements in SWM practices in Class I cities in India. The report was incorporated with the recommendations for improving SWM practices in Class I cities in the country and making cities clean and liveable. It was this committee who recommended the Government to make the rules under Environment Protection Act which resulted into promoting the Solid Waste (Management and Handling) Rules in 2000 which included support measures that should be extended from Central and state governments for effective strategy planning.

3.5.C. THE NATIONAL ENVIRONMENTAL POLICY, 2006

---

[144] Report of the High Power Committee Urban Solid Waste management in India, Planning Commission Government of India 1995
[145] GOOD GOVERNANCE AND SOLID WASTE MANAGEMENT: AN OVERVIEW OF LEGISLATIVE REGULATIONS IN INDIA Vaishali Gupta, Sushma Goel, T. G. Rupa
[146] Almitra H Patel v. Union of India (1998) 2 SCC 416

In 2006, 'The National Environment Policy, 2006' recognised the importance and contribution of ragpickers in recycling industries and recommended in the action plan that "Give legal recognition to, and strengthen the informal sector systems of collection and recycling of various materials. In particular enhance their access to institutional finance and relevant technologies."[147]

3.5.D. THE PERFORMANCE AUDIT ON "MANAGEMENT OF WASTE IN INDIA, 2007

In the year 2007, the Performance Audit on "Management of Waste in India, 2007 was released by the Comptroller Auditor General of India. While recognising the immense contribution of waste pickers to managing waste in the country, the 2007 Audit Report is highly critical of the Ministry of Forests and Environment for providing no legal protection to waste pickers in India. The audit clearly states that "MoEF had not appropriately addressed the role of informal sector in handling waste. Only 17 *per cent* of the sampled states had recognised the role of ragpickers. [Paragraph 3.5.1 & 3.5.2] "recognising the importance of ragpickers in the recycling industry.[148]

---

[147] National Environment Policy 2006, Government of India Ministry of Environment and Forests.

[148] Report of the Comptroller and Auditor General of India for the year ended March 2007, Report No. PA 14 of 2008

3.5.E. NEW SOLID WASTE MANAGEMENT RULES

"Ministry of Environment, Forest and Climate Change had comprehensively revised and notified Solid Waste Management (SWM) Rule in April, 2016 in supersession of the Municipal Waste (Management and Handling) Rules, 2000. As per these rules,

"According to the new Rule 11(1) (c) explicitly recognises and acknowledges the primary role played by the ragpickers in recycling."[149]

"Rule 15 of the SWM now makes it mandatory for all local bodies to formulate new and broad guidelines to create a facility for the rag pickers."[150]

"Further Rule 11(1) (m), also makes it mandatory to start a registration scheme for Rag pickers."[151]

"Rule 3(1)(31) also makes it mandatory for the municipalities to provide a 'Material Recovery Facility 'where Rag pickers may segregate, sort and store recovered wastes."[152]

---

[149] SWM RULES 2016 (July 13,2020. 04:04 AM)
http://bbmp.gov.in/documents/10180/1920333/SWM-Rules-2016.pdf/27c6b5e4-5265-4aee-bff6-451f28202cc8
[150] Ibid
[151] Ibid
[152] Ibid

The above committees in India have explicitly dealt with the welfare of ragpickers. We can clearly see that all the committee clearly recognises the importance of ragpickers in the recycling unit and calls for the creation of a law to recognise and to protect the ragpicker.

Further the committees also recognises the health hazard of the ragpickers and also urge government to provide the protective gears to them and to engage the ragpickers in capacity building and skill development program.

The committees also additionally add and request social workers and the environmental activist to form the associations and welfare organisations for the ragpickers to empower them and to protect them.

3.5.F. PUNE AND THE RAGPICKERS

'There are 3540 SWACH waste pickers in Pune and 580 registered KKPKP waste pickers in PCMC.'[153] They provide an essential service of waste collection to 10, 00,000 households or more than 40, 00,000 individuals. 'The rest of the 3000 informal and itinerant KKPKP waste pickers rely solely on the daily sale of recyclables for their income.[154] Their work benefits the health of the city and supports the city's solid waste management, yet they are unprotected due to the informal nature of their work. Many of

---

[153] KKPKP, (July 1,2020 02:04 AM) http://kashtakaripanchayat.org
[154] Ibid

them simply cannot afford to suspend their work to protect their health. Totally, there are around 7,000 waste pickers working in Pune and PCMC every day, providing an essential service and keeping the cities clean.'[155]

3.5.G. ASSOCIATIONS AND ORGANISATIONS

"Kashtakari Panchayat is a registered trust in 2010 which primarily to support the rag pickers and their families. They offer their help in the way of direct financial assistance to the indirect support in the form of training, facilitation and research. The main objects of KPT are to provide training and technical support to them, to provide social and educational help to the ragpickers, to advocate for the rights of the workers, and to try and improve the livelihood of ragpickers."[156]

The association had fought many battles for the rights of the ragpickers, has managed to give sorting shades, health benefits or the educational benefits or the other social security benefits to the rag pickers.

3.5.H. MAHARASHTRA AND SOLID WASTE MANAGEMENT.

'Maharashtra is the only state to have registered its own brand "Harit Maha City Compost" for promotion of marketing and sale of

---

[155] Ibid
[156] Id

city compost which is as per the FCO standards and SWM Rules 2016.' [157] 'Urban Local Bodies have integrated rag pickers into formal system and involve them for recycling and recovery of waste. Rag pickers are provided with identity cards, basic facilities and personal protective equipment.' [158]

"State of Maharashtra is very active in the solid waste management treatment Maharashtra has topped the list of municipal solid waste generators in the country in 2018, according to data from the Ministry of Housing and Urban Affairs (MoHUA) submitted to the union environment ministry. Maharashtra generates 82.38 lakhs metric tonnes (MT) of waste an annum or 22,570 MT waste a day, of which 44% is being treated."[159]

This shows us that the State of Maharashtra does have a comprehensive legal framework for dealing with the solid waste management as well as the legislative competence to make laws that would provide a boost to the same.

---

[157] Implementation of Solid Waste Management Rules, 2016, FOR THE STATE OF MAHARASHTRA, Maharashtra pollution control Board -2018. Page no. 3

[158] Ibid. Page no. 4

[159] HindustanTimes, Maharashtra top most solid waste generator in India. https://www.hindustantimes.com/mumbai-news/maharashtra-topmost-solid-waste-generator-in-india-in-2018/story-gBaHAupqW1cShdM2OihWzJ.html.

CHAPTER 4
DATA ANALYSIS

INTRODUCTION

Pune is the second-largest city in the state of Maharashtra.[160] It has been marked as number one city for the ease of living index.[161] Pune has been ranked 10th, in the list of the cleanest cities in India.[162] In 2006, The National Environment Policy, recognised the importance and contribution of ragpickers in recycling industries and recommended in the action plan that there should be legal recognition to the informal sector who work in collection and recycling process to strengthen them and to enhance the financial and relevant technologies.[163]

Ragpickers are the most responsible labours for picking the scraps and other recyclable wastes, which act as raw material for the industries in Pune, by doing so they save corers of rupees. The ragpickers who are not much educated, work in the unhygienic conditions are exposed to the maximum health hazards. Ragpickers

---

[160] City Census Department, About City Census, (Nov.19,2019, 12:20 AM) https://pmc.gov.in/en/about-city-census.
PMC, (July 13,2020. 04:04 AM) https://pmc.gov.in/en/about-city-census
[161] Maps of India, Top ten wealthiest towns of India, (Nov.19,2019, 01:02 AM)https://www.mapsofindia.com/top-ten-cities-of-india/top-ten-wealthiest-towns-india.html.
[162] Swatch Survekshan survey -2018
[163] National Environment Policy 2006, Government of India Ministry of environment and forests.

also have an association named as *Kashtakari Panchayat* to fight for their rights. Rag picking is being recognised by the government. The government has given employment to most of the ragpickers by giving the contracts to any private associations or by hiring them in the municipal associations. However, only those ragpickers are hired, who are provided with the Identity cards or other benefits guided by SWM rules. There are more than 3000 ragpickers in the Pune city who are uncertified and who don't have any Identity Cards but are still there in this business. Not only the ragpickers who are adult but there are also ragpickers who are children and still are engaged in this business violating the provisions of Child Labour Act.

"Bhaskar Majumdar and G Rajvanshi in their paper have clearly mentioned that children from 5-17 years of age are also associated with this work. This can be seen because they are often deprived of the education or are excluded from the childcare. These children work on daily basis to enhance their household income, notwithstanding the Act on child labour that makes it a punishable offence."[164]

Ragpickers are known as 'Kachra wala, kabadi wala or ghanta gadi wala or Bhangarwala 'in the local Slang. Rag pickers have recently been recognised by the government in the SWM

---

[164] Supra Note 26, Bhaskar Majumdar and G Rajvanshi.

rules and various committees. Among the studies conducted and the surveys done, it was found out that the majority of the ragpickers are women and children. The study done by the women in informal employment globalising and organising Integrating Waste Pickers into Municipal Solid Waste Management in Pune, India by Poornima Chikarmane [165] cites the socio-economic profile of the ragpickers form the Pune. The data shows that there are 90% women ragpickers in the occupation and 90% of the ragpickers are illiterate without having any social security with most of the serious health hazards. 50% of the Rag pickers work for more than 9 hours and more than 50% of the ragpickers are more than 35 years of age.

4.1. EMPIRICAL STUDY:

A field study has been conducted in the area of the Pune city mainly Prabhat Road, Yerwada, Lohgaon and Vadgaon localities. Pune being one of the cleanest cities in India is supposed to serve as exemplars to the other Municipal Corporations. Here, the attempt was made to assess and to analyse the difficulties and predicaments of the community engaged in the Rag picking occupation.

4.2. SAMPLING METHOD AND SAMPLING SIZE

Random data sampling method is used for carrying out the interviews with a total size of 10 ragpickers, including men and women of varied age group, actively involved in the rag picking

---

[165] Supra Note 77

business. The interviews were aimed at seeking from the respondents, details regarding their age, education, work experience, health hazards, and awareness of the social security schemes among other things. All interviewers participated voluntarily and without any compensation whatsoever. Further, it is hereby submitted that the reliability of the present research report is solely based on the consistency of the opinions expressed by the respondents.

4.3. IMPORTANCE OF EMPIRICAL SURVEY

The empirical study is done by the researcher to support and to validate or invalidate the doctrinal research done by the researcher and to give a practical and realistic base for the answers to the research questions. Researcher's main object behind this research was to understand the need of health insurance for the Ragpickers. The purpose of the research was to understand the level of awareness of the public health insurance schemes and problems relating to accessing and utilising the benefits of public health insurance schemes. The present study is conducted in Pune and a Total of 10 Ragpickers who was above the age of 18 years was selected for this study. A descriptive study is conducted by face to face interviews.

4.4. ANALYSIS OF PRIMARY DATA

Question 1. Age Group

The data clearly shows that 40% of the respondents belonged to the more than 50 years of age, followed by the 30% of respondents who belong to the age group of 30 to 50 years. The remaining 30% belong to the age group of 18 to 30 years

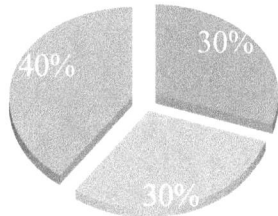

respectively.

Figure 1. **The above Figure shows the Age Group of the Respondents**

Above figure clearly shows that maximum ragpickers engages in this occupation are above 50 years of age and by calculations, we come to the conclusion that more than 70% of the ragpickers are more than 30 years of age. Rag picking is more of a physical work, and we can imagine that a person above 50 years of age walking for than 5 hours a day and working for more than 8 hours a day, will definitely suffer from any health issues.

The above figure also clearly indicates that rag picking occupation is majorly done by the people who are above 50 years of age and 30% by the people who are above 30 years of age and below 50 years of age.

The remaining 30% from 18 to 30 years of age group making rag picking a mixed occupation which is done by any age group. However, some calculations indicate that 70% of the ragpickers are more than 30 years of age, thereby making rag picking an occupation of the mid aged to old age people. The other surveys have also found out that the child ragpickers are also associated with this business, but in this research the researcher has focused more on the ragpickers who are above the 18 years of age.

Question 2: Gender

The data shows that 60% of the respondents are men and 40% of the respondents are women. The survey clearly shows that there are more men engaged with this occupation than the number of females. However, many other surveys have cleared showed that female ragpickers are mostly associated with the fixed type of rag picking, where male are mostly associated with *Itinerant Buyers* type of rag picking. These are the ragpickers who purchase recyclables from the other ragpicker and then resell them up the chain for an added value.

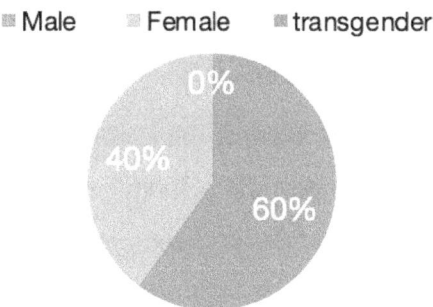

Figure 2. The above Figure shows the Gender of the Respondents

The main object behind asking this question was to analyse the gender role in the rag picking occupation, where it was found out that there are more numbers of male ragpickers who are engaged in the business. However, the study did by the women in informal employment globalising and organising Integrating Waste Pickers into Municipal Solid Waste Management in Pune, India by Poornima Chikarmane (2001) shows that there are 90% of the women ragpickers associated with this business. The researcher does not denies the doctrinal research because it also suggests that itinerant buyer type of rag picking is mostly done by the males and over the years the sector has seen a rise in the number of men. The data analysed reveals that 60% of the ragpickers in the business are men.

Question 3: What is your Education?

After focusing on age and gender, the researcher has focused on the educational qualification of the respondents so that it is easy to understand the illiteracy rate in this occupation. .

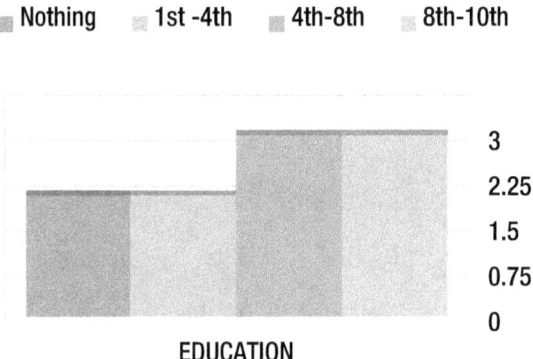

The above figure clearly shows that: only 3 ragpickers out of 10 have studied more than 8th standard. The other 3 have studied upto 8th standard, the 2 studied till 4th standard and remaining 2 did

not study at all. The data clearly shows that ragpickers have basic educational qualification which can help them in their daily life. The basic education can be a source of life in today's era, because the
basic education can help them to understand the social security schemes or the other government policies which are proposed for them.

As discussed in the report of Chikarmane (2001) surveys suggests that 90% of the ragpickers are illiterate, or the survey by G. Siva Praveena, Ch. Durga Prasad, Prof. P.V.V. Prasada Rao (2015) suggests that 62% of the ragpicker do not have any basic education. The research does not agree to those researchers per se, because according to the survey conducted by the researcher, most of the ragpickers have basic or primary education which can help them to understand or help them to read and write in their daily life which does not make them illiterate.

Question 4: Where are you from?
In this question, researcher has focused on the native place of the respondents so that it is easy to understand whether there is any migration pattern in the occupation.

The data clearly shows that 70% of the ragpickers are migrated from the rural to urban areas in search of employment,

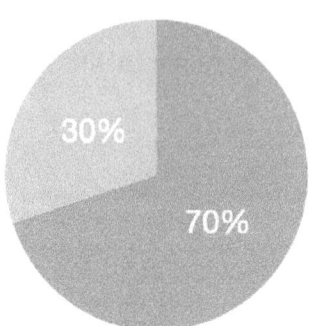

**Figure 4.
The above Figure shows the Migration Status
of the Respondents**

while 30% of the ragpickers were from the Pune city that landed up in this business voluntarily.

Papiya Sarkar (2003)[166] in their paper had talked about the migration status of the unorganised workers. The paper says that 97.5% of the ragpickers are migrant but in the survey done by the researcher, he initially got the answer that 70% of the respondents are migrated and 30% are non migrated. The researcher agrees completely to the survey done by the Papiya Sarkar in his report, because majority of the ragpickers are migrated, and face similar problems which are

---

[166] Supra Note 60, Papiya Sarkar

the domiciles of the state or the domicile of the district. They face problems in availing the benefits of social security schemes which are provided by the state government.

Question 5: How long you are been in this occupation?
Researcher framed this question to understand the nature and importance of the experience in the rag picking occupation.

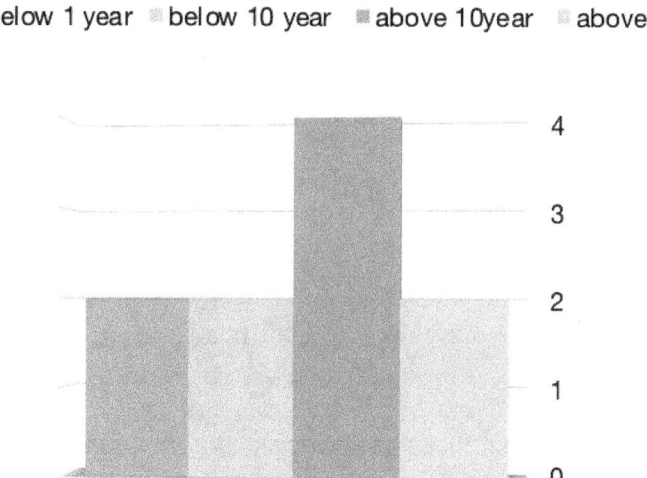

Figure 5. The above Figure shows the Occupational Experience of the Respondents

The above data reveals that 4 out of 10 ragpickers had an experience of 10years and above. 2 out of 10 ragpickers had more than 20 years of experience. The other 2 out of 10 are new, whereas the remaining 2 out of 10, have an experience of below 10years. The main motive of this question was to understand the role of experience in the rag picking business, so that we can link the experience to the wages of the ragpickers.

As the ragpickers who mainly deals with the metal or plastic things get more income rather than the ragpickers who collect papers or other materials. It is observed that the experienced ragpickers work for the less time and earn enough amount of money. It is also observed that experienced ragpickers collect only those materials which give them a good amount of money and do not waste their time with inexpensive things which fill their bags. The above data shows that rag picking is done by the people for more than 20 years and experience of the ragpickers in the business is partially linked with their income or working hours.

Question 6: How long do you work in a Day?

The researcher's main object to ask this question was to understand the ratio of working hours of the ragpickers so that it gives a clear idea to the researcher about the connection between long working hours and the health status of the ragpickers. The purpose was also to understand the connection between working hours and the income of the Ragpickers.

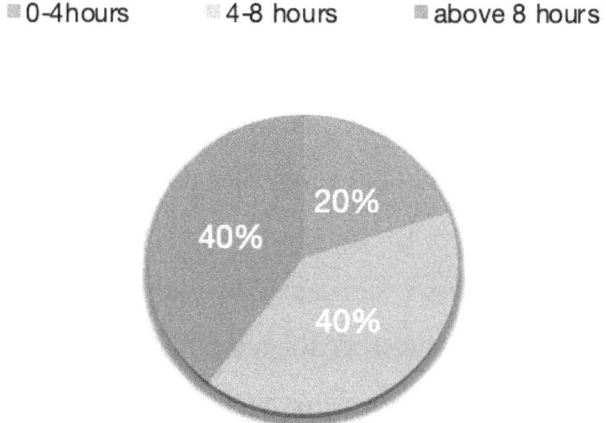

Figure 6. The above Figure shows the working Hours of the Respondents

The above data shows that 4 out of 10 ragpickers were working for more than 8 hours a day and other 6 out of 10 were working from 8 to 12 hours respectively. The data clearly shows that there is no fixed working hours for ragpickers.

Rag picking is any time occupation and does not have any fixed working hours. Many other surveys have found out that there are also ragpickers who work in midnight as there are more chances to collect expensive rags before any other rag picker. Rag picking is not the occupation which can only be done in a fixed time but it can be done at any time. The Rag pickers are mostly self-employed and so, they can work at the time feasible to them. However, the same is not the condition with the ragpickers who are working under any association. They have to work for the specific time which is fixed by the employer and have all rules like an employee of organised sector.

The report of Chikarmane (2001) clearly states that 75% of workers walk for more than 5 hours daily and 50% of workers work for 9-12 hours daily. The researcher does not agree with the report because over the years, this sector has seen many changes in their livelihood. The survey conducted by the researchers suggests that 40% of the ragpickers work for more than 8 hours a day, the other 40% of the ragpickers work upto 8 hours a day and the remaining 20% work upto 4 hours a day. The data analysed reveals that most of the ragpickers work upto 8 hours a day which is a lot of physical work which can affect their health condition as clearly pointed out by the report of Chikarmane (2001).

Question 7: For which organisation you are working?

The above mentioned question is to understand the status of ragpickers in various organisations under which they are working

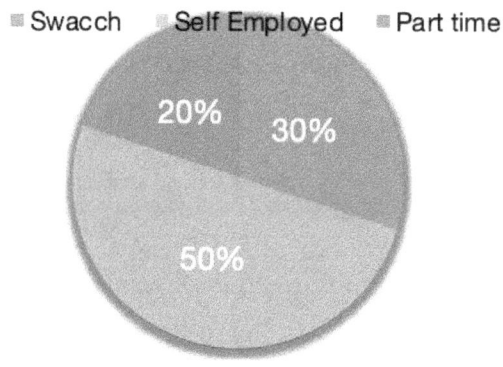

Figure 7. The above Figure shows the Organisation for which the Respondents are working

The above data shows that 50% of the ragpickers were self employed, 30% were working for the Swatch organisation and remaining 20% ragpickers were involved in rag picking business as part time workers who worked as watchmen. The analysis reveals that the rag pickers choose to work separately rather than to work under any association.

The ragpickers who are working for any organisation have to work as the employees of organised sector, and get an monthly salary and bonuses as the organised sector workers but the ragpickers who are working as the self employed don't have any such benefits like the organised ragpickers or are not even aware of the benefits for which they are eligible. The ragpickers who are self employed are totally depended on the amount and quality of the rag they collect while the ragpickers who work for any association get paid monthly. In spite of this, the researcher in the survey found out that ragpickers choose to be self employed rather than working for any organisation. It has been also found out by this survey that self employed ragpickers work for the junkyard dealers who help them if needed.

It has been found out by the surveys by the WIEGO Policy Brief (Urban Policies) N8 July 2012 in Integrating Waste Pickers into Municipal Solid Waste Management in Pune, India that most of the ragpickers are self employed and also recognises the part time ragpickers. The survey also shows the research of KKPKP which plans to provide Identity Cards to each and every ragpicker in Pune. The researcher completely validates the survey done by the WIEGO and agrees to it over the point that most of the ragpickers choose to be self employed rather than working for any association.

Question 8: What are your wages?

The above mentioned question is focused on the wages of ragpickers and is asked to understand the socio-economic condition of the ragpickers.

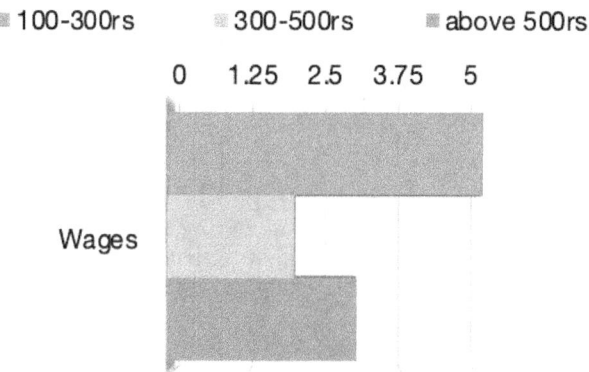

Figure 8. The above Figure shows

The above figure shows that 50% ragpickers earned up to 300 /- rupees per day. While the other 20% earned up to 500 /- and the remaining 30% earned above 500 /- rupees in the rag picking occupation. The above data shows the economic condition of the ragpickers by their daily wages.

Mostly rag pickers are the poor workers in the unorganised sector, and the above data shows that 50% of the ragpickers hardly earn up to 300 rupees a day which hardly goes to Rs. 9000 per month. This is the amount with which they have to fulfil their daily needs. However, many other surveys found out that ragpickers live in the slums and have 4 or 5 members to feed in their family. They hardly earn to match their daily expense. So, we can conclude that the ragpickers are very poor workers in the unorganised sector. The data also shows that the ragpickers who act as a dealers earn more money by doing less work. The data also shows that most of the ragpickers who are self employed earn more than the ragpickers from any organisation. The data analysed also shows that ragpickers belongs to very poor class of the society and if at all they have to bear the hospital expenses then they cant fulfil the daily expenses and it will become hard for them to eat their daily bread.

In this regards the survey done by the Pinky Chandran, Nalini Shekar, Marwan Abubaker and Akshay Yadav[167] shows that 70% of the ragpickers earn up to Rs 200 in a day and 18% of the ragpickers earn more than 200 Rs a day. In comparison to which,

---

[167] Supra Note 42, Pinky Chandran, Nalini Shekar, Marwan Abubaker, Akshay Yadav .

the survey done by the researcher clearly states that 50% of the ragpickers earn up to Rs 300 and 20% earn up to 500 rupees per day and the remaining 30% earn more than 500 rupees a day. The data analysed reveals that 50% of the ragpickers in Pune earn up to rupees 300 and other 50% of earn more than that. However, considering the working hours and the physical work in which the ragpickers are engaged, the overall daily expenses and the other miscellaneous expenses, we can imagine the socio economic condition of the ragpickers.

Question 9: Is there any other family member involved in the same business (If yes, then specify)?

The question mainly focuses to know the involvement of any other family member who is doing the same occupation. This question was to understand the nature of the occupation and to get a clear understanding of the rag-picking as an occupation.

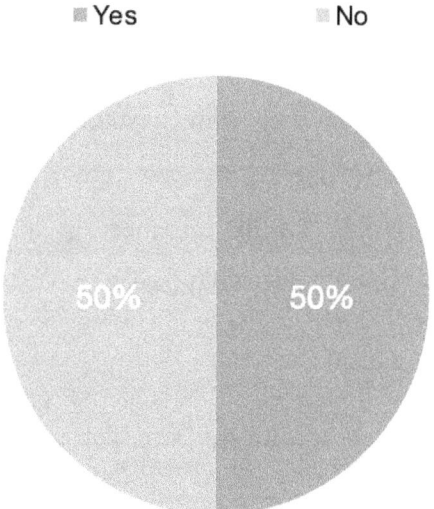

Figure 9. The above Figure shows that involvement of family members in the same business.

The above figure shows that out of 10 ragpickers 5 ragpickers had their family member involved in the same occupation and other 5 responded that they don't have any family member involved in this occupation. The above data shows that rag picking is not the family business and is done by the member in the family or sometimes any one member of the family is involved in the same occupation but whole family is not involved in the same occupation.

In this regards survey done by the Shaheda Niloufer, A. V. V. S. Swamy, K. Syamala Devi [168] shows that 94.73% of the ragpickers are assisted by the family members in this occupation. The survey done by the researcher found out that 50% of the ragpickers have their family assistance and engaged in the same business, and remaining 50% of the ragpickers did not have any family assistance or another family member engaged in the occupation. The data analysis reveals that rag pickers do not necessarily involve their family members in the same business making the rag picking a family business.

---

[168] Shaheda Niloufer , A. V. V. S. Swamy ,K. Syamala , In Waste Collection by Rag Pickers in the Cities – A Brief Report Devi , Volume : 2 | Issue : 4 | April 2013 ISSN - 2250-1991 , PARIPEX - INDIAN JOURNAL OF RESEARCH

Question 10: Are you aware of any of these health insurance schemes which are provided by the government?

The question is a very direct and focuses on to analyse the knowledge of ragpickers regarding the health insurance schemes.

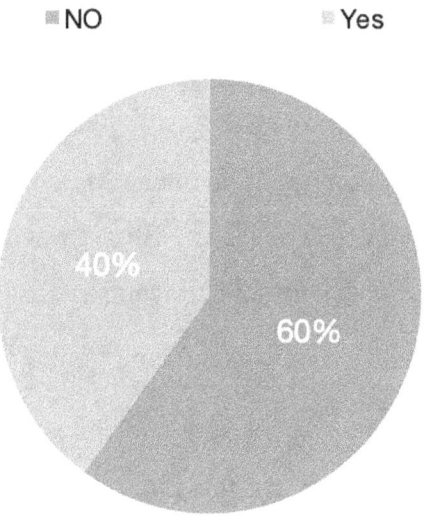

Figure 10. The above Figure shows the Percentage of Awareness about the health insurance scheme to the Respondents

The above data shows that 60% of the ragpickers responded to this question in negative. as they are not aware of the health insurance schemes which are provided by the government while 40% of them knew about the health insurance schemes. The data shows that ragpickers are not aware about the health insurance schemes.

It is clearly seen by the above data that the majority of the ragpickers are not aware of the social security schemes. The survey also helped researcher to understand that the ragpickers who are working under any organisation are aware about the health insurance schemes but the ragpickers who are self employed are unaware of such social security schemes. Many surveys have found out that the ragpickers are often found treating their wounds by applying the limestone (CHUNA) or by tying their wounds by a dirty cloth which results in a serious infection sometimes, this is only because the people try to avoid visiting hospitals.

In this regards survey done by Balu Natha Mote, Suhas Balasaheb Kadam, Shrikant Kishorrao Kalaskar, Bharat Shivajirao Thakare, Ambadas Suresh Adhav, Thirumugam Muthuvel[169] clearly shows that ragpickers 75% of the ragpickers don't go to any public health check up camps are unaware of health hazards . To the comparison in which researcher have framed this direct question to understand the percentage of awareness about the health insurance to which 60% of the respondents did not know about any health insurance scheme. The data analysis reveals that ragpickers are not aware

---

[169] Supra Note 46, Balu natha mote, Suhas Balashaeb kadam, Shrikant Kishorrao kalakar, Bharat Shivajirao Thakare, Ambadas Suresh Adhav, Thirumugam Muthuthuvel,

about the social security schemes specially the health insurance schemes.

Question 11: Do you know the following health insurance schemes which are provided to the Ragpickers?

The question is framed in this way because many a times people utilises the benefits but don't know what it is called as or what the name of the scheme is. The main object of this question was to understand and analyse the health insurance schemes which are mostly used or which the ragpickers are aware of.

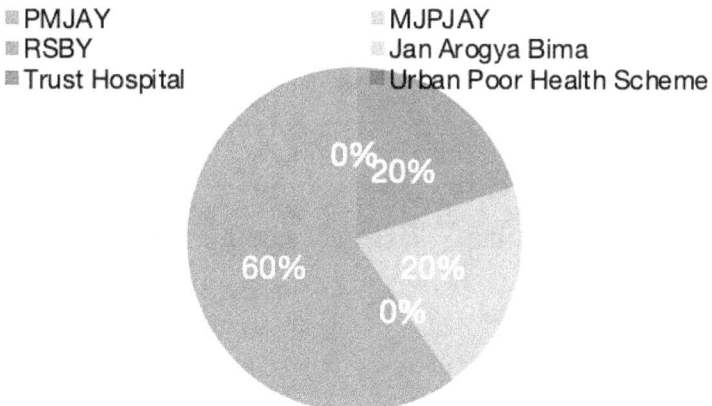

Figure 11. The above Figure shows the awareness of the mentioned Health Insurance schemes

The above data shows that 60% of ragpickers responded in negative to this question as they were unaware of any of the health insurance scheme which was suggested to them the remaining 40% of the ragpickers were aware about 2 schemes. The analysis shows that ragpickers are unaware of the policies and the social security schemes are failing in their motives of covering the eligible sector. The health insurance schemes are not properly advertised and do not reach to the eligible sector. This results in the ragpickers going to the general practitioners, by spending money from their pockets and making their socio economic condition worst.

Question 12: Are you a beneficiary to any of this scheme?

The question mainly focuses on understanding the utilisation of the scheme, as many a time's people are aware of but don't utilise the benefits from the scheme for many reasons. The question number 11 analyses the awareness of the social security and question number 12 analyses the utilisation of the insurance schemes.

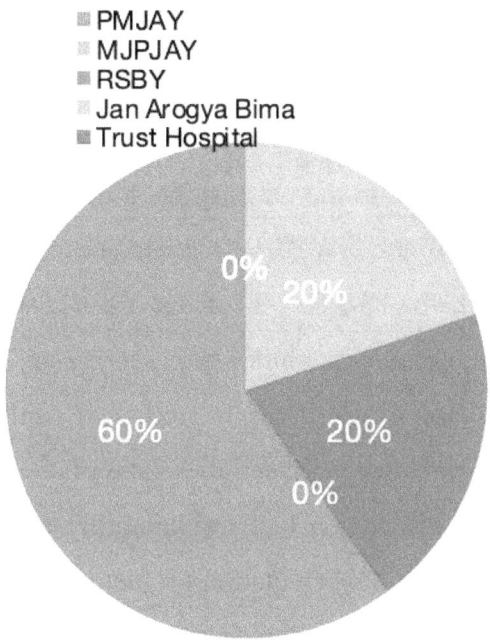

Figure 12. The above Figure shows the Beneficiary Respondents to any mentioned scheme

The data clearly shows that only 40% of the ragpicker knew about the health insurance schemes. The 2 ragpickers out of 4 who knew about the health insurance schemes were associated with the Swatch organisation and the other 2 were self employed and were young and educated up to 10th. The others were unaware of any of the health insurance scheme and were visiting the general private practitioner when needed.

The researcher by the survey also found out that ragpickers preferred visiting trust hospitals rather than going to the public hospitals due to the service they provide. It was also found by the doctrinal research from the Occupational Health of Waste Pickers in Pune: KKPKP and SWaCH Members Push for Health Rights Ujjwal Samarth for KKPKP, 2014 that trust hospital always find an excuse and ploys to shirk their responsibility towards the patients who cannot afford the full costs of healthcare. KKPKP *karyakartas*/members have faced these and other typical situations which included the reason like unavailability of beds or IPF are exhausted or for the documentation problems or getting tests done form outside which costs ragpickers a lot. In comparison to this, the researcher has also found similar cases doing the research where ragpickers mostly complained about the documentation problems for availing the benefits or the excuses which hospital staff gave. The researcher completely agrees with the research and confirms the loopholes in the social security schemes, and the reasons for not utilising the health insurance scheme.

Question 13: If not then what are the reasons?

The question mainly focuses upon checking the views of the respondents, as to why they don't utilise the benefits of the scheme even when they are aware of the schemes.

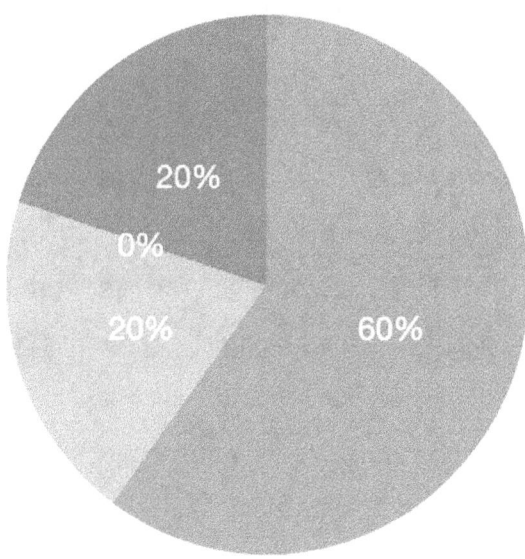

Figure 13. The above Figure shows the Reason for not being the Beneficiary to any of the scheme

The above data shows that 60% of the ragpickers responded that they are not aware about the health insurance scheme. Out of the remaining 40%, the 20% did not need a health insurance scheme and the other 20% were the beneficiary to the government health insurance scheme.

The research clearly states that ragpickers do not utilise the benefits from the health insurance schemes because most of them are unaware of the health insurance scheme or the process on how to avail it. If some are aware of the health insurance schemes then they don't want to avail the benefits form it because of the loopholes in it. Many surveys have clearly pointed out the loop holes in the various insurance schemes. One of the papers, which the researcher has come across was *The Occupational Health of Waste Pickers in Pune: KKPKP and SWaCH Members Push for Health Rights Ujjwal Samarth for KKPKP, 2014*. The paper clearly shows the loopholes in the various health insurance schemes. The paper shows the loopholes of the trust hospitals and Jan Arogya health insurance scheme which are utilised by the remaining 40% of the ragpickers who utilises the benefits from the health insurance schemes. The data analysis clearly states that ragpickers are not aware to the health insurance schemes and if they are aware then such incidents of the loopholes of the social security schemes stop them from utilising the health insurance benefits.

Question 14: What problems do you face when you visit the hospitals?

The researcher had focused on this question regarding the problems of the ragpickers when they go to the hospitals because it helps the researcher to know the current condition of the public health services.

Researcher's motive to keep this question open ended was to understand the problems of the ragpicker, so that it can help researcher to come out with the suggestions for them and to learn the drawbacks of the social security scheme on ground level.

Ragpickers complained that public hospitals have very long procedures and fixed timing for everything. Long procedure included that when they first visit the hospital they have to pay the hospital fees and have to take prescription slip. After that they have to go to the respective rooms, where the speciality doctor is available. In complying with both of these procedures, they have to stand in long queues before the doctor diagnosis the ragpicker. The doctor prescribes some test for which, they have to stand again in the long queues. Here, they have to pay the fees of prescribes test and after that they have to take that slip and to go to respective test room where once again they have to stand in long queues. After the test, they again have to wait for the reports and after that they have to go to the doctor once again. This once again requires them to stand in queue and then finally doctor prescribes the medicine. In this long procedure, the ragpickers cost their day and have to take a work off from the work. This does not end here and they have to pay the extra fees for the test, according to the charges. In this process, if the ragpicker wants to avail any social security benefit, then they have to show the qualifying document for the required scheme, but such required documents are not readily available with the ragpicker so even if they are the eligible for the social security benefits they cannot avail the benefits from the scheme. It was also pointed out by the ragpickers that they face the problem of discrimination while standing in the queues or while being diagnosed by the doctor or by the hospital staff.

To analyse the data, the main problems when ragpickers visit the hospital can summed up to the poor services by the hospitals, long queues, unnecessary procedures, documentations for availing the social security benefits, discriminations faced from the hospital staff. These problems are also pointed out by many surveys.

Question 15: What are the health hazards in your daily Activities?

The question is framed very directly to understand the health hazards which they face in their daily lives. This will help the researcher to understand the need for health insurance to the ragpickers?

The open ended question allowed research to know the problems and health hazards in detail the main health hazard which researcher notices was the injuries which ragpickers get.
Ragpickers get cut them self by the glass or steel or any other sharp objects. Ragpickers also inhale the harmful gases which cause them breathing problems. Almost every ragpicker is bitten by the dogs or any other stray animals. Common cold or cough is a very common problem. Almost all the ragpickers suffer from the musculoskeletal problem. They have to take long walks or have to carry or push the long carts which cause many problems. A lot of ragpickers face the problems of the skin diseases or the gastro tract infection or the respiratory tract infections, or eye problems or any

substance abuse diseases or water borne diseases including kidney stones or typhoid. This is the daily health hazards which are faced by the ragpickers.

Ragpickers being more engaged in unhygienic occupation are always exposed to such diseases, but this is because the ragpickers do not have any protective gears to protect themselves from such diseases. They are not given any training to protect themselves from such hazards. In this regards, the survey done by Balu Natha Mote, Suhas Balasaheb Kadam, Shrikant Kishorrao Kalaskar, Bharat Shivajirao Thakare, Ambadas Suresh Adhav, Thirumugam Muthuvel[170] clearly shows the diseases to which ragpickers are more prone to and the percentage of ragpickers which are affected by such diseases. The researcher completely agrees to the suggestions and the need of health insurance and for providing protective gears to the ragpickers.

Question 16: Problems for maintaining Hygiene?

The question focuses to understand the problems they face in maintaining their hygiene.

Infections or health hazards to which ragpickers are more exposed to are caused due to not maintaining the proper hygiene. The researcher through the survey found out that in most of the

---

[170] Supra Note 46, Balu natha mote, Suhas Balashaeb kadam, Shrikant Kishorrao kalakar, Bharat Shivajirao Thakare, Ambadas Suresh Adhav, Thirumugam Muthuthuvel,

cases public toilets are not available in many wards, sorting shades are not available in many wards, there are no public drinking water dispensers in the ward, and if they are available they are not cleaned. The sorting shed or public washrooms are never cleaned by the municipalities; sanitary pads for female ragpickers are not provided at the sorting shed or the public washrooms. Ragpickers face this problem on regular basic to maintain their personal hygiene.

The data analysis shows that there are serious problems faced by the ragpickers for maintaining the personal hygiene but this are because the municipalities are not doing their job to clean the public toilets and to provide water dispensers. Such problems result in serious threats to ragpickers by infecting them with the GTI or RTI infections or other Urinary tract infections or skin diseases or water borne diseases. These are some serious threats which are caused due the unhygienic environment. In the survey done by Papiya Sarkar[171] clearly mentions these serious threats in their paper.

---

[171] Supra Note 45, Papiya Sarkar

Question 17: How many times do you visit the hospital in a year?

The question is focused mainly to understand the ratio or frequency of going to the hospital.

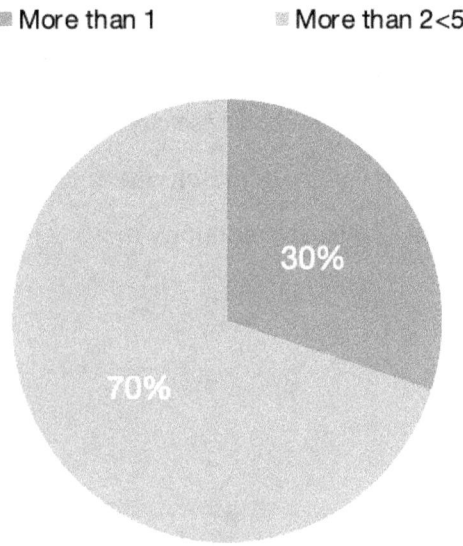

Figure 14. The above Figure shows the percentage of Utilisation of Public Hospitals

The above data shows that approx 70% of ragpickers visit hospital more than 2 and less than 5 times in a year and the remaining 30% of the ragpickers visit up to 2 times in a year. It shows the utilisation of the hospitals by the ragpickers.

The data clearly shows the degree of utilisation of the public hospitals but if to compare it with the awareness of the health insurance schemes or the problems faced by the ragpicker during the hospitalisation, clearly states the expenses they make during their hospital visit. The degree of utilisation of public hospitals is much less than the health hazards they have.

The survey done by the Balu Natha Mote, Suhas Balasaheb Kadam, Shrikant Kishorrao Kalaskar, Bharat Shivajirao Thakare, Ambadas Suresh Adhav, Thirumugam Muthuvel clearly states that the ragpickers go to the private general practitioners mostly and visits only public hospital when it costs more in the private hospitals. The researcher completely agrees to the survey done by them, and analyses that the degree of utilisation of public hospitals is much less than they visit the private hospitals.

Question 18: What are the approximate expenses on hospital bills?

The question aims to understand the approximate expenses of

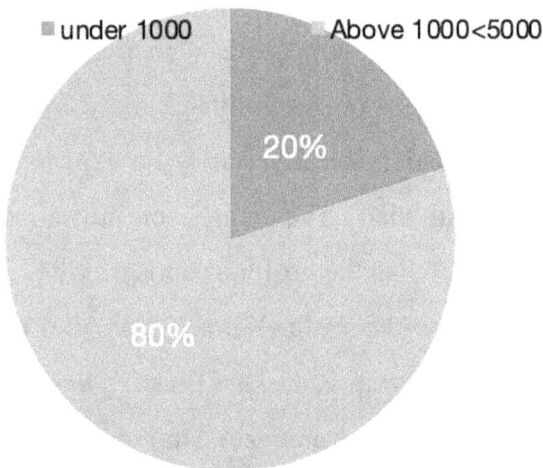

Figure 15. The above Figure shows the approx out of pocket expenditure of the Respondents

hospital bills to the ragpickers.

The figure shows that 80% of the ragpickers spend Rs. 1000 – Rs. 5000, at the hospital. The data also shows that 20% of the ragpickers spend up to 1000 rupees at the hospital. The data reveals that the ragpickers, who merely earns their bread, spend a large amount of money in the hospital bills.

Maximum ragpickers hardly earn up to 9000 rupees a month in which they have to feed their family and have to save for the future contingencies. If from this amount, they have to spend such a huge amount for the hospital bills, it is way too hard for them. Many surveys show that for minimising such expenses ragpickers mostly avoid going hospitals.

Question 19: Are you the part of any union or association which is fighting for the rights of the ragpickers?

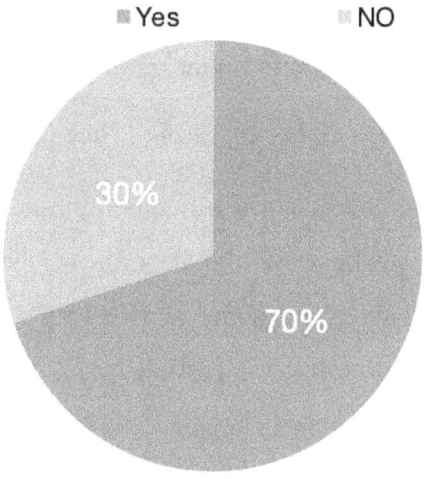

Figure 16. The above Figure shows the Percentage of Respondents connected with

Lastly, this question was framed by the researcher to analyse the seriousness of the associations and unions among the ragpickers, which are fighting for their rights.

The above data shows that 70% of the ragpickers are associated with one or another association which is working for their rights. 30% of the ragpickers are not associated with the association. The data shows that 70% of the ragpickers are seriously associated with the associations who are working for their class.

It clearly states that ragpickers associations are successfully connecting most of the ragpickers under one roof and are fighting together for their rights. "The researcher has found out that KKPKP is the registered association which is fighting for the rights of ragpickers and is working for the benefits of the ragpickers. Kagad Kach Patra Kashtakari Panchayat (KKPKP) has been the holder of Jan Arogya Group Insurance Policy (JAP) of New India Assurance Company (NIA) since January 2003. The premium for the policy is paid by the Pune Municipal Corporation from its annual budget SWaCH has worked with both Tata Motors and students from MIT design school in Pune to redesign some of the equipment used by waste collectors–specifically the push carts, *aakdis* (spear/sticks used to poke and pick up waste) and sacks. KKPKP had filed RTI for the information on the trust hospitals for providing the bed and other benefits to the ragpickers, associations carry the health awareness programs or capacity building programs for the ragpickers."[172] Researcher completely agrees to the importance of associations and unions fighting for the rights of the ragpickers.

4.5. CONCLUSION:

Rag pickers are the class of the workers in the unorganised sector, who play an important part in the Indian economy and in the recycling chain. Ragpickers are the important chain of the recycling unit. After conducting an empirical study, the researcher has tried to gauge the opinions of the ragpickers over it. The researcher has come to realise that it is rather convenient to feel a sense of sympathy towards this class of the workers. The hazards they face and the work they do is nearly impossible for all of us to fill their shoes. The government has taken a lot of initiatives to protect them and to promote them by recognising the importance of ragpickers and the health hazards they are exposed to in their daily lives. But the ragpickers are not aware of the social security schemes they are eligible for or to which they are the beneficiaries. The social security schemes which are provided to them have a major loophole in it and they have failed to reach to their eligible

---

[172] Ujwala Samarth for KKPKP, The Occupational Health of Waste Pickers in Pune: KKPKP and SWaCH Members Push for Health Rights ,2014

beneficiaries, this is the major loophole in the any social security scheme which is provided to them.

The study was intended to understand the need for health insurance to the Ragpickers and to understand the problems relating to accessing and utilising the benefits of public health insurance schemes.

CHAPTER 5

CONCLUSION AND RECOMMENDATIONS

The study was intended to understand the need of health insurance for the Ragpickers, understanding the problems relating to accessing and utilising the benefits of public health insurance schemes. Ragpickers are the workers from the organised-unorganised sector who work for long hours and work in unhygienic conditions and are more prone to infections and many other health hazards. This compromises their immunity, which results in fatigues and making them more prone to acquire many diseases.

Based on the studies undertaken, the following conclusions are drawn

Ragpickers are not aware of the social security's which are provided to them. The major loophole in the social security schemes is the awareness of that scheme. The schemes are failing because they are not readily available to the eligible beneficiaries. Ragpickers being vulnerable community cannot afford to pay for the insurance schemes or hospital bills. Providing free insurance will help them. When they go to the hospitals, the discrimination they face is known to us by the survey and many other reports have also drawn these things. The long queues and the time required in the public hospital shows the poor services of the public hospital which mostly fails to bring such poor and vulnerable workers to the hospitals. The failure of municipalities in providing clean drinking water and hygienic public toilet also shows the failure of local governments to protect not only the ragpickers but the general public too.

There are many laws which prevent other unorganised sector workers from the exploitation and provide many work benefits to them. To name a few there are Inter-State Migrant Workmen (Regulation of Employment and Conditions of Service) Act, 1979, the Building and Other Constructions Workers' (Regulation of Employment and Conditions of Service) Act, 1996, and the Beedi Workers Welfare Fund Act, 1976, the Cine Workers and Cinema Theatre Workers (Regulation of Employment) Act, 1981, the Mica Mines Labour Welfare Fund Act, 1946, the Dock Workers (Safety, Health and Welfare) Act, 1986. However, there is no separate law or welfare recognition for the ragpickers. The SWM rule 2016 recognises the ragpickers and has some provisions in it which talks about the ragpickers and the benefits from them.

Ragpickers being the vulnerable workers, have to work in unhygienic conditions and have to face the occupational health hazards or the shortage of infrastructure or the sorting sheds or the social security's, Solid Waste Management Rules 2016, have framed some rules which should be followed by the respective local government bodies. The rules clearly indicate that there should be a formal integration of the ragpicker bodies. The material recovery centres should be provided to them and protective gears should be provided to them or any other form of support which would empower ragpickers.

RECOMMENDATIONS

It is recommended by the researcher that these recommendations should be considered in the existing guidelines for the welfare of the ragpickers.

- Rights and requirements of the ragpickers can be addressed as a legal obligation instead of an optional mechanism.

- While conducting the survey the researcher has come across the health hazards and problems of the ragpickers to which the researcher recommends that; the state government must ensure that the social protection, labour protection, or capacity building programmes are organised for the ragpickers.

- Based on the above evaluation of problems and difficulties of the rag pickers and their need for health insurance, the researcher recommends the following clauses in the existing set of guidelines :

1. It is imperative to consider the importance of identification of the ragpickers to expect the utilisation of social security schemes by the eligible beneficiaries. Hence, the state government ought to take up the duty of appointing local officials to take all necessary steps for identifying all the individuals working in this sector. The survey conducted by the

researcher clearly shows that ragpickers mostly choose to be self employment rather than working for any private organisation. Therefore, these self employed ragpickers do not have any identification cards to show their occupation and have no other document to avail the social security benefits. Hence, researcher recommends that appointing any local officials for identification of such ragpickers can prove to be an efficient step to cover and identify all the individuals in the rag picking business.

2. A major barrier in utilising the scheme or availing the benefits of the scheme; by the ragpickers is awareness. The survey done by the researcher clearly shows that ragpickers are not aware about the health insurance schemes which are provided to them and those who know are facing many problems to avail the benefits from those schemes. The major problem which researcher noticed was the problem of the documentation. The income certificates, the caste certificates or the domicile certificates ragpickers are not readily available with the ragpickers. Therefore, identifying the ragpickers by a government process and providing them the identification certificate in the Form of the Permanent Identity Card can help the ragpickers. Hence, researcher recommends that social security benefits could be provided on producing such identification certificate which can be in the form of Permanent Identity Card. The researcher also recommends that more focus

must be given on spreading the awareness of the scheme and on the process of availing it.

3. Further, after the identification process and providing the identification certificates by the government is complete, the government must ensure that protective gear, first aid kits, or other advanced gears are distributed regularly to the ragpickers.

4. It is also recommended that Local government must ensure that sorting sheds would be well equipped with sanitary pads, clean drinking water and adequate toilet facilities.

5. The survey conducted by the researcher it has come to notice of the researcher that ragpickers often face discrimination by the hospital staff, the policemen, the society guards or the general public. The researcher strongly recommends that government must take strict action against such officials or the general public for the welfare of ragpickers.

6. Further, the researcher also recommends that Government must ensure that the skill training and capacity building programmes, awareness programmes, health checkup camps, counselling sessions must be carried out by the local government. Ragpickers can develop their skills so that they can earn more money. Health camps, awareness camps or the counselling sessions must be carried out on the regular basis so that ragpickers can be made aware of the health hazard or the social security schemes.

7. Further, the researcher also recommends that the state government ought to create body under the department of Labour to ensure the welfare benefits to the ragpickers.

8. The survey carried out by the researcher clearly shows that NGOs or the self help group helps the ragpickers in many ways. Therefore, initiatives must be taken by the municipalities to encourage the ragpickers to form associations, unions or setting up NGOs or the self help groups which can help them for solving social, financial, executive or mental problems.

9. Further, the private ragpicker organisations and associations must spread awareness about the social security schemes to the eligible beneficiaries. The terms and conditions must also be included in the contracts given by municipal bodies to such associations for flowing the social security benefits to the eligible beneficiaries.

10. Lastly and more importantly, the researcher strongly recommends that steps must be taken to educate the child ragpickers by encouraging them for education. This can be done by giving them scholarships or other benefits.

The Government should take all these factors into account and should take steps to protect the one of the most vulnerable and important community as a matter of urgency.

BIBLIOGRAPHY

1. Akhileshwar reddy, Alok Prasanna Kumar, Waste pickers welfare law in Karnataka,
2. Ar. Jepranshu Aganivanshi, The Rag Pickers and the Urban Economy – A Case Study of Seemapuri region, Delhi ,International Journal of Research in Social Sciences, ISSN: 2249-2496
3. Bhaskar Majumdar and g Rajvanshi, migrating to rag picking : unfolding some facts about child rag pickers in the city of Allahabad, Uttar Pradesh, Manpower Journal,Vol.LINo.4,October-December 2017
4. Caroline Hunt ,Child waste pickers in India: the occupation and its health risks ,Environment and Urbanization, Vol. 8, No. 2, October 1996
5. Chandramohan, C. Ravichandran ,V. Sivasankar , Solid waste, its health impairments and role of rag pickers in Tiruchirappalli city, Tamil Nadu, Southern India , http://www.sagepub.co.uk/journalsPermissions.nav ISSN 0734–242XWaste Management & Research 2010: 28: 951–958 DOI: 10.1177/0734242X09352705 ,
6. G. Siva Praveena Ch. Durga Prasad Prof. P.V.V. Prasada Rao , The Plight of Rag-pickers at Dump yard Socio - Economic Profile A Case Study of Visakhapatnam ,

7. G. Siva Praveena Ch. Durga Prasad Prof. P.V.V. Prasada Rao, The Plight of Rag-pickers at Dump yard Socio - Economic Profile a Case Study of Visakhapatnam, ISSN: 2454-5988, Cointreau, Sandra. 2006. "Occupational and Environmental Health Issues of Solid Waste Management: Special Emphasis on Middle and Lower-Income Countries." Urban Papers 2, World Bank, Washington, DC. Dhuy, Eloise. 2008.
8. Gender Dimensions of the Informal Sector and Informal Employment in India.
9. general principles of law of insurance , R.N.Chaudhary
10. International Labour Organization International Programme on the Elimination of Child Labour (IPEC)
11. Investigating the Worst Forms of Child Labour No. 4 Nepal Situation of Child Ragpickers: aA Rapid Assessment
12. K. P. Kannan & T. S. Papola, Workers in the Informal Sector: Initiatives by India's National Commission for Enterprises in the Unorganized Sector (NCEUS), 146 Int'l Lab. Rev. 321 (2007).
13. National Commission for Enterprises in the Unorganised Sector
14. Poornima Chikarmane and Laxmi Narayan Organising the Unorganised: A Case Study of the Kagad Kach Patra Kashtakari Panchayat (Trade Union of Waste-pickers)

15. Poornima Chikarmane, Integrating Waste Pickers into Municipal Solid Waste Management in Pune, India, WEIGO POLICY BRIEF
16. Report On Rapid Assessment Survey On Socio-Economic Condition Of Waste Pickers In Kolkata Municipal Area, society for Direct Initiative for Social and Health Action (DISHA)
17. Reports On Financing Of Enterprises In The Unorganised Sector & Creation Of A National Fund For The Unorganised Sector (NAFUS), National Commission for Enterprises in the Unorganised Sector
18. Shaheda Niloufer, A. V. V. S. Swamy, K. Syamala, In Waste Collection by Rag Pickers in the Cities – A Brief Report Devi, Volume : 2 | Issue : 4 | April 2013 ISSN - 2250-1991, PARIPEX - INDIAN JOURNAL OF RESEARCH
19. Solid waste, its health impairments and role of rag pickers in Tiruchirappalli city, Tamil Nadu, Southern India, A. Chandramohan, C. Ravichandran and V. Sivasankar.
20. T. N. Krishnan, Hospitalisation Insurance: A Proposal, Economic and Political Weekly, Vol. 31, No. 15 (Apr. 13, 1996), pp. 944-946
21. Tara Mc Closkey, Shantha Parthan, Sameer Prasad, MALNUTRITION IN RAG-PICKER COMMUNITIES, XVI Annual Conference Proceedings January, 2015 ISBN no. 978-81-923211-7-2

22. The Challenge of Employment in India An Informal Economy Perspective Volume I - Main Report
23. The ILO and the Informal Sector an institutional history
24. Ujwala Samarth for KKPKP, The Occupational Health of Waste Pickers in Pune: KKPKP and SWaCH Members Push for Health Rights

WEBLIOGRAPHY

1. http://kashtakaripanchayat.org
2. http://righttoeducation.in/know-your-rte/about
3. http://socialjustice.nic.in/SchemeList/Send/24?mid=24541
4. http://swachcoop.com/pdf
5. http://www.businessworld.in/article/Richest-Cities-Of-India/28-06-2017-121011/
6. http://www.internationalconference.in/XVI_AIC/INDEX.HTM
7. http://www.kkpkp-pune.org/charitable-trust-hospitals.html
8. http://www.prsindia.org/uploads/media/Unorganised%20Sector/bill150_20071205150_National_Commission_on_Labour_2_Chapter_7_unorganised_sector_Part_A.pdf
9. http://www.rsby.gov.in/how_works.html
10. http://www.sagepub.co.uk/journalsPermissions.nav
11. http://www.wiego.org/sites/default/files/publications/files/Dias-Samson-IEMS-Waste-Picker-Sector-Report.pdf
12. https://economictimes.indiatimes.com/news/politics-and-nation/centre-to-start-award-for-ragpickers-from-next-year-prakash-javadekar/articleshow/47616122.cms?from=mdr

13. https://nlsenlaw.org/solid-waste-management-an-indian-legal-profile/
14. https://pmc.gov.in/en/about-city-census
15. https://pmc.gov.in/pmc-web
16. https://pmjay.gov.in/about/pmjay
17. https://pune.gov.in/scheme/sanjay-gandhi-yojana/
18. https://rmoneyinsurance.com/blogs/life-insurance/importance-insurance-must-know/
19. https://timesofindia.indiatimes.com/city/mumbai/Rag-pickers-most-vulnerable-to-sexual-assault-NGO-says/articleshow/22218955.cms
20. https://unstats.un.org/unsd/gender/Ghana_Jan2009/Doc41.pdf
21. https://www.acko.com/health-insurance/
22. https://www.acko.com/health-insurance/aam-aadmi-bima-yojana/
23. https://www.bankbazaar.com/life-insurance/jan-arogya-bima-policy.html
24. https://www.bankofbaroda.in/atal-pension-yojna.htm
25. https://www.economist.com/asia/2007/11/15/scavenger-hunt
26. https://www.escr-net.org/caselaw/2019/municipal-council-ratlam-v-shri-vardhichand-others-1980-air-1622-1981-scr-1-97
27. https://www.firstpost.com/author/indiaspend

28. https://www.firstpost.com/health/covid-19-could-become-endemic-like-hiv-and-may-never-go-away-who-expert-mike-ryan-8366961.html
29. https://www.hindustantimes.com/mumbai-news/maharashtra-topmost-solid-waste-generator-in-india-in-2018/story-gBaHAupqW1cShdM2OihWzJ.html
30. https://www.ibef.org/economy/economic-survey-2018-19
31. https://www.indiatimes.com/news/india/ragpickers-are-our-unsung-heroes-in-keeping-india-clean-high-time-govt-starts-caring-for-them-378820.htm
32. https://www.irdai.gov.in/ADMINCMS/cms/Uploadedfiles/NEWINDIA15/
33. https://www.jeevandayee.gov.in/MJPJAY/FrontServlet
34. https://www.mapsofindia.com/top-ten-cities-of-india/top-ten-wealthiest-towns-india.html
35. https://www.policyx.com/health-insurance/articles/rashtriya-swasthya-bima-yojana-rsby/
36. https://www.who.int/emergencies/diseases/novel-coronavirus-2019/advice-for-public
37. https://www.wwfindia.org/?13287/People-for-Transparency-Through-Kamal-Anand--Vs--State-of-Punjab-Ors

www.ingramcontent.com/pod-product-compliance
Lightning Source LLC
Chambersburg PA
CBHW050012230526
45465CB00003BB/1380